WHO IS MUHAMMAD'S GABRIEL?

Kent A. Philpott, MDiv, DMin

EVM
Earthen Vessel Media, LLC

WHO IS MUHAMMAD'S GABRIEL?
©2022 by Kent Philpott

All rights reserved.
Earthen Vessel Media, LLC
San Rafael, CA 94903
www.earthenvesselmedia.com

ISBN: 978-1-946794-35-2 print
        978-1-946794-36-9 eBook

Library of Congress Control Number: 2022930509

Cover and interior design by KLC Philpott

No part of this publication may be reproduced, stored in a retrieval system, or transmitted in any form or by any means, electronic or mechanical, including photocopying, recording, or by any information retrieval system, without the written permission of the author or publisher, except by a reviewer who wishes to quote brief passages in connection with a review written for inclusion in a magazine, newspaper, internet site, or broadcast.

All Biblical Scripture quotations, unless otherwise indicated, are taken from the Holy Bible, English Standard Version® (ESV®), copyright© 2001 by Crossway Bibles, a publishing ministry of Good News Publishers. All rights reserved.

Contents

A Special Appeal to Muslim Readers	V
Introduction	6
Who Is Gabriel?	8
A Follower of Muhammad? A Follower of Jesus?	24
Were the Crusaders and Inquisitors Christians?	27
Looking at Muslims	36
A Fundamental Error of Islam	39
The Weakness of Islam	41
Islam's Cultic Connection	44
My First Essay on Islam	53
Shame versus Guilt	57
Abrogation or Progressive Revelation?	62
Eid Al-Adha: Who Has it Right?	69
The Making of an Extremist	74
But, It Is Warfare!	80
Muslim Honor Brigades	84
Sexual Repression in Islam	87
Why the Taliban Enforces Strict Islamic Law	90
I Am Not Anti-Muslim	94

A Special Appeal to Muslim Readers

Some of what you will find in this book may upset you. If I were Muslim, I would be offended at some points I make in this book, and especially with the first essay, "Who is Muhammad's Gabriel?"

My appeal to you is to have the courage to read the difficult passages. Finding truth and reality is far more important than protecting ourselves from sharp challenges.

Faith must be anchored in ultimate truth and not in traditions. Christians face this on a constant basis, with the result that it makes us stronger. So then, dear Muslim reader, my hope and prayer are that you will have the strength and courage to look at material that will likely contradict what you believe.

Introduction

The lead essay, "Who is Muhammed's Gabriel?" may be a difficult read for Muslim people, and it is to Muslim people across the globe that this book is written.

The essays in this book were written over a twenty-year period, and the reader will notice differences in my orientation or feelings toward Islam in some compared to others. Many years ago, I developed a love for Muslim people, and this especially after the tragedy of September 11, 2001, and after coming to personally know several Muslims from a nearby community. The more I learned about Islam and especially the more I engaged with Muslim people directly, my views softened, in that I realized Muslims were caught in the vice grip of an exceedingly unhealthy religious system.

For two years, 2018 to 2020, Imam Abu Qadir Al-Amin of the Muslim Community Center in San Francisco and I talked with each other—not debated, rather communicated together about what and why each believed—in a television program series. We remain friends and speak with each other on occasion. You can view these television programs by going to milleravenuechurch.org/watch-our-tv-shows.

One of the dividing lines in Islam is fervor, in that the Islam of the extremists is purer, more traditional, and more radical than that practiced and understood by moderates. Only a small percentage of Muslims know much about their religion; the zealous Muslim knows more about Islam, makes it his business to study and be guided by ardent elders, and understands that to have a chance of going to paradise rather than hellfire, it is necessary to be a very fervent follower of Islam.

Most Muslims want to live and let live. But their entire identity, their worldview, is Muslim. They cannot imagine being anything but Muslim.

Outreach to Muslims is then dependent on the miracle working of God; the new birth is from above. It cannot be argued into them or coerced.

To be clear, I see Islam as wrongly oriented and founded. I no more accept Islam as a revelation from God than I do Hinduism, Buddhism, Shamanism, and the belief systems of many neo-pagan groups.

All organized religions are flawed, including Christianity. I am a Baptist pastor who understands that Baptists are flawed as well. Any and every institution with humans involved will be corrupt to some measure, some more than others. I believe that God was in Christ reconciling the world to Himself and that God sent His only Son to take our sin upon Himself—to die, be buried, and be resurrected. He will come again to judge the living and the dead. There is salvation in none but Jesus Christ of Nazareth.

To repeat: the lead piece to this small book of essays may be upsetting to Muslims. I know this, as I have visited our local Sunni Mosque for many years now. It is possible that some there will read this and not be pleased with me or feel that I am against them, even despise them, none of which is the case. My overarching view is that people who embrace Islam are people whom the God and Father of our Lord Jesus Christ loves, and they are people for whom Jesus shed His blood on the Cross.

This grouping of short essays may also be of value to those who wish to understand the main tenants of Islam. It reflects what I learned during my years of researching this world religion. Feel free to contact me at kent@milleravenuechurch.org with questions or comments.

ESSAY 1

WHO IS GABRIEL?

This essay will examine three questions. First: Who is Gabriel? The answer prompts a second question: Who is Allah? The answers to these provoke a third question: Who is Muhammad? All that is Islam hangs on the answers to these three questions.

GABRIEL OF THE BIBLE

The name Gabriel is found in four places in the Bible: Daniel 8:16 and 9:21, and Luke 1:19 and 1:26. The name Gabriel means, "God is mighty."

FIRST, THE TWO PASSAGES FROM THE OLD TESTAMENT BOOK OF DANIEL:

> When I, Daniel, had seen the vision, I sought to understand it. And behold, there stood before me one having the appearance of a man. And I heard a man's voice between the banks of the Ulai, and it called "Gabriel, make this man understand the vision." (Daniel 8:15-16)

> While I was speaking and praying, confessing my sin and the sin of my people Israel, and presenting my plea before the LORD my God for the holy hill of my God, while I was speaking in prayer, the man Gabriel, whom I had seen in the vision at the first, came to me in swift flight at the time of the evening sacrifice. (Daniel 9:20-21)

Gabriel is thus introduced in the Book of Daniel, and we see more of him in the New Testament.

SECOND, THE TWO PASSAGES FROM THE NEW TESTAMENT GOSPEL OF LUKE

While the priest Zechariah was on duty at the Temple in Jerusalem, an angel of the Lord appeared to him. The angel announced to Zechariah that the prayers of him and his wife Elizabeth had been answered to the effect that Elizabeth would bear a son and his name would be John. We pick up the story in Luke chapter 1:

> *And Zechariah said to the angel, "How shall I know this? For I am an old man, and my wife is advanced in years." And the angel answered him, "I am Gabriel who stands in the presence of God and I was sent to speak to you and to bring you this good news." (Luke 1:18-19)*

> *In the sixth month the angel Gabriel was sent from God to a city of Galilee named Nazareth, to a virgin betrothed to a man whose name was Joseph, of the house of David. And the virgin's name was Mary. (Luke 1:26-27)*

Now we look at the words of Gabriel to Mary in verse 28: *"Greetings, O favored one, the Lord is with you!"* Mary, greatly troubled at the greeting, tried to understand what the angel meant. Gabriel continued:

> *"Do not be afraid, Mary, for you have found favor with God. And behold, you will conceive in your womb and bear a son, and you shall call his name Jesus. He will be great and will be called the Son of the Most High. And the Lord God will give to him the throne of his father David, and he will reign over the house of Jacob forever, and of his kingdom there will be no end." (Luke 1:30-33)*

Is the angel in Matthew also Gabriel?

Joseph, about to marry Mary to whom he was betrothed, was troubled when he learned she was pregnant. Thinking to divorce her quietly, he had a visit from an angel while in a dream. The angel (no name given) said to him:

> *"Joseph, son of David, do not fear to take Mary as your wife, for that which is conceived in her is from the Holy Spirit. She will bear a son, and you shall call his name Jesus, for he will save his people from their sins." All this took place to fulfill what the Lord had spoken by the prophet: "Behold, the virgin shall conceive and bear a son, and they shall call his name Immanuel" (which means, God with us). When Joseph woke from sleep, he did as the angel of the Lord*

commanded him; he took his wife, but knew her not until she had given birth to a son. And he called his name Jesus."

Is the angel who spoke to Joseph the same one who spoke to Zechariah and Mary? We cannot be completely sure, but it seems as though it must be the case. However, the argument I am about to make does not depend on the answer to that question, as both angels in Luke and in Matthew are clearly angels of the Lord.

What have we learned so far?

The angelic appearances have to do with the birth of Jesus, the one who would save His people from sin. The birth was miraculous, accomplished by the Holy Spirit, and this is all the explanation for the pregnancy we have. The point is clear: no human being had sex with Mary. Neither God the Father nor God the Holy Spirit had sex with Mary. The birth was miraculous, and this fits perfectly with the word God revealed to Isaiah six hundred years earlier:

> *Therefore, the Lord himself will give you a sign. Behold, the virgin shall conceive and bear a son, and shall call his name Immanuel. (Isaiah 7:14)*

The passage is referred to as "The Sign of Immanuel," meaning that the virgin's child is God come to be with us in a miraculous, non-human manner—thus a sign. God actually became flesh, which the Creator of the universe could do. And He did.

The child born to Mary was not called Immanuel but Jesus. Immanuel, in traditional Jewish understanding, is what He, Immanuel, is, which is God become man. The name Jesus refers to what He would *do*. "Jesus" is a word derived from the Hebrew name for Joshua. It means, "God saves." Joshua was the one who brought the Chosen People across the Jordan River into the Promised Land of Canaan. Moses would not be allowed to do this, and the concept is that the Law of Moses cannot bring salvation. No, salvation is a gift of God and is not by works of the Law. In His dying for sin, Jesus became the Savior, and this is proven by His resurrection. Jesus is Immanuel, God with us.

One last word from Gabriel, the angel of the Lord

Gabriel said to Mary in reference to the child she would bear: *"He will be great and will be called the Son of the Most High" (Luke 1:32).* This virgin birth, not the result of sexual intercourse, would be miraculous. The child would be of the same nature as the Father.

Then Gabriel said, *⁵He will reign over the house of Jacob forever, and of his kingdom there will be no end" (Luke 1:33).* The meaning is obvious—the child will be the reigning King forever, just as Isaiah had announced:

> *"For to us a child is born, to us a son is given, and the government shall be upon his shoulder, and his name shall be called Wonderful Counselor, Mighty God, Everlasting Father, Prince of Peace" (Isaiah 9:6).*

Without question, the Prophet Isaiah states that the child born is God Himself.

This takes us into the mystery of the Trinity. We will never fully comprehend how the Father, the Son, and the Holy Spirit are one and complete God all at once. Christian historians and theologians simply note what the evidence reveals.

The point is plain enough—the child born is God in the flesh. He is Jesus born of the virgin in Bethlehem, the one who would die in our place, taking our sin upon Himself, then on the third day be raised from the dead. He is alive now in heaven, one day to return to receive His own.

Nearly six hundred years later, however, there appeared another "Gabriel."

GABRIEL OF ISLAM

The majority of Muslims today hold that the Qur'an is eternal (eternal as Allah is eternal), was brought down to earth by an angel, and was then recited by the angel Gabriel to Muhammad. Allah spoke each and every verse to the angel who then recited them, piecemeal, over the course of about twenty-two years, to Muhammad. Muhammad, unable to write, memorized the recitations and spoke them to others, who then wrote them down. (Qur'an means recitation, or that which is recited.)

The angel that appeared to Muhammad at a cave on the slopes of Mount Hira near Mecca, about 610 CE, also had the name Gabriel. It was the custom of many Jews, Christians, Zoroastrians, and Gnostics to retire to secluded places in hopes of receiving spiritual dreams and visions and thereby experience a direct connection with deity. Muhammad was one of these.

Ascetics would fast, meditate, and stay awake for days in order to empty the mind and receive dreams and visions. Muhammad, after a time, achieved trance-like states during which the angel Gabriel, as the angel announced himself to Muhammad, spoke to him. We find a hint of this in the hadith of Abu Dawud, Book 12, No. 2247a, which reads, "When the Apostle of Allah (peace be upon him) came to himself (after the revelation ended) ...."

Muhammad reported his visits by Gabriel to his wife Khadija, who supported the idea that it was indeed an angel speaking to her husband. Though Muhammad was not sure of the nature of the vision he had, he eventually adopted his wife's opinion.

At the very beginning of Muhammad's encounter with Gabriel, he wondered if he was actually in contact with a jinn (demon) rather than an angel. This is stunningly apparent based on a hadith reported by Aisha (the mother of the faithful believers and favorite wife of Muhammad) as found in the most trusted of all hadiths, Sahih Al-Bukhari, Vol. 1, Book 1, No. 3:

> The commencement of the Divine Inspiration to Allah's Apostle was in the form of good dreams, which came true like bright day light, and then the love of seclusion was bestowed upon him. He used to go in seclusion in the cave of Hira where he used to worship (Allah alone) continuously for many days before his desire to see his family. He used to take with him the journey food for the stay and then come back to (his wife) Khadija to take his food likewise again till suddenly the Truth descended upon him while he was in the cave of Hira. The angel came to him and asked him to read. The Prophet replied, "I do not know how to read."

The Prophet added, "The angel caught me (forcefully) and pressed me so hard that I could not bear it anymore. He then released me and again asked me to read and I replied, 'I do not know how to read.' Thereupon he caught me again and pressed me a second time till I could not bear it anymore. He then released me and again asked me to read but again I replied, 'I do not know how to read (or what shall I read)?' Thereupon he caught me for a third time and pressed me, and then released me and said, 'Read in the name of your Lord, who has created (all that exists) and has created man from a clot. Read! And your Lord is the Most Generous.

Muhammad was so harshly treated by what he thought was the angel

Who Is Gabriel? 13

Gabriel that he doubted it was an angel from Allah at all. He became depressed and considered throwing himself off the mountain of Hira. It was only through the intervention and convincing of Khadija, his first wife, that Muhammad was prevented from doing so.

There is an interesting account referred to as "The Lap." The story is that Muhammad continued to believe the being that appeared to him was a jinn, a demon. Khadija, in the midst of Muhammad's fears and doubts, asked him to sit on her lap, first one side then the other. When he did, she asked him if he saw the angel. He responded, yes. Then she asked him to again sit on her lap and once again asked if he saw the angel. Again, yes. Then she disrobed and asked Muhammad to sit on her lap again. She asked if he saw the angel, and Muhammad said, no. With that Khadija convinced Muhammad it was indeed the angel Gabriel by saying that only a good angel would not look upon a woman's nakedness.

The above account is a paraphrase from the Sira, the official biography of Muhammad. Below now is the account, called "The Lap" as reported by Ibn Ishaq, Muhammad's biographer:

> Ibn Ishaq recorded that when the spirit came to Muhammad another time, Khadija tested him:
>
> Ishma'il b. Abu Hakim, a freedman of the family of al-Zubayr, told me on Khadija's authority that she said to the apostle of Allah, 'O son of my uncle, are you able to tell me about your visitant, when he comes to you?' He replied that he could, and she asked him to tell her when he came.
>
> So when Gabriel came to him, as he was wont, the apostle said to Khadija, 'This is Gabriel who has just come to me.' 'Get up, O son of my uncle,' she said, 'and sit by my left thigh.'
>
> The apostle did so, and she said, 'Can you see him?' 'Yes,' he said. She said, 'Then turn around and sit on my right thigh.' He did so, and she said, 'Can you see him?' When he said that he could she asked him to move and sit in her lap.
>
> When he had done this she again asked if he could see him, and he said yes, she disclosed her form and cast aside her veil while the apostle was sitting in her lap. Then she said, 'Can you see him?'

And he replied, 'No.' She said, 'O son of my uncle, rejoice and be of good heart, by Allah he is an angel and not a satan.

(Ibn Ishaq, The Life of Muhammad, tr. Guillaume, 1967, p. 107)[1]

GABRIEL IN THE QUR'AN AND HADITH

Gabriel appears in only three verses in the Qur'an: Sura 2:97-98 and Sura 66:4.

Say, (O Muhammad, to mankind)[2] : Who is an enemy to Gabriel! For he it is who hath revealed (this Scripture) to thy heart by Allah's leave, confirming that which was (revealed) before it and a guidance and glad tidings to believers. Sura 2:97

Who is an enemy to Allah, and His angels and His messengers, and Gabriel and Michael! Then, lo! Allah (Himself) is an enemy to the disbelievers. Sura 2:98

If ye twain turn unto Allah repentant, (ye have cause to do so) for your hearts desired (the ban); and if ye aid one another against him (Muhammad) then lo! Allah, even He, is his protecting Friend, and Gabriel and the righteous among the believers; and furthermore, the angels are his helpers. Sura 66:4

THE GABRIELS: SAME OR DIFFERENT?

Of incredibly significant importance is the question: Is the Gabriel of the Bible and the Gabriel of Islam one and the same?

The reader, of course, will be alerted that I am going to make the case that the two are different, in fact, very different. However, it is easy to be fooled. The apostle Paul warned the Church at Corinth that demons could disguise themselves as angels:

---

1   The *Sira* has for centuries been linked with the Qur'an and hadith as authoritative on the life of Muhammad. In more recent years the *Sira* has been largely neglected, as the accounts of what Muhammad said and did are rather fantastic, problematic, and embarrassing.

2   Words in parentheses-( )-indicate explanatory notes made by editors of the Qur'an. Without them so very many passages of the Qur'an would be unintelligible.

For such men are false apostles, deceitful workmen, disguising themselves as apostles of Christ. And no wonder, for even Satan disguises himself as an angel of light. So it is no surprise if his servants, also, disguise themselves as servants of righteousness. Their end will correspond to their deeds. (2 Cor. 11:13-15).

Let me be clear: the Gabriel of the Bible and the Gabriel of the Q'uran are both angels. One is an angel of the Lord; the other is a fallen angel, a demon. My contention is that a fallen angel—a jinn or demon—appeared to Muhammad on Mount Hira. Muhammad was right in his first assessment.

THE ULTIMATE OFFENSE

To state that Islam's Gabriel is a jinn is to state the ultimate offense for Muslims, since it utterly negates the big three: Allah, the Qur'an, and Muhammad. Allah, because it is Allah who is relaying to Gabriel what is in the Qur'an. Then Gabriel is no angel but a demon. And Muhammad is merely passing along what a demon is reciting to him. Islam is then based upon absolute error, even deception, and nothing more.

Such accusations, let alone suggestions, can earn one the death penalty in Muslim-majority societies. Religions or governments that forcefully, even ruthlessly, stifle dissent show their weakness. This is true of Islam, even in countries where the Muslim population is small. If a Muslim abandons Islam, which is called apostasy, he or she may be punished by death, though this is not clearly spelled out in the Qur'an.

THE CHRISTIAN'S OBLIGATION

With the understanding of this enormous deception, what must a Christian do? Must we remain silent and not voice even the possibility that the whole of Islam is based on demonic deception? To refrain from speaking out is immoral and unethical.

Writers of Scripture were known for denouncing false religion and the behaviors they spawn. Many paid the ultimate price for standing with the truth. Many are dying today in Muslim-dominated nations for speaking their hearts and minds.

In the face of terror and considering the great commission given Christians by Jesus Himself (see Matthew 28:19-20, among others), it is necessary to stand up to the murderous lying of the chief demon, Satan.

Jesus, while countering the attacks of religious opponents, was clear. Jesus said:

> *You are of your father the devil, and your will is to do your father's desires. He was a murderer from the beginning, and has nothing to do with the truth, because there is no truth in him. When he lies, he speaks out of his own character, for he is a liar and the father of lies.* (John 8:44)

It is not disrespectful to challenge error, especially when the difference is between heaven and hell, both of which are eternal.

ANOTHER ISLAMIC TEACHING ABOUT GABRIEL

Some spokesmen for Islam identify Gabriel as the Holy Spirit in both the Bible and the Qur'an. From where in Islam's authoritative texts do they get this? In Sura 2:87 and Sura 2:253, and without the word Gabriel appearing, we find, "We supported him with the Holy Spirit." Islamic interpreters say this "We" is the angel Gabriel. But the plain text of the Qur'an does not state this.

Not only does the Qur'an not identify Gabriel with the Holy Spirit, but neither does the hadith. Instead, we find just the opposite, as illustrated by Sahih Muslim, in book 30: "Gabriel, the Apostle of Allah is among us, and the Holy Spirit who has no match." Gabriel is not the Holy Spirit.

THE HOLY SPIRIT IN THE BIBLE

THE HEBREW BIBLE

Both the Hebrew Bible and the New Testament show the nature and identity of the Holy Spirit. The Holy Spirit is deity, often referred to as the Spirit of God, in that the Holy Spirit is holy, and only God is holy. The Holy Spirit is omnipresent, is referred to as a "He" and thus is personal, and is omnipotent, meaning all powerful. And the Holy Spirit can only be God as are the Father and the Son.

The second verse of Genesis speaks of the Holy Spirit being involved at the moment of the creation of the universe. *"The earth was without form and void, and darkness was over the face of the deep. And the Spirit of God was hovering over the face of the waters."*

2 Samuel 23:2-3 identifies the God of Israel with the Spirit of the LORD:

The Spirit of the LORD speaks by me; his word is on my tongue. The God of Israel has spoken; the Rock of Israel has said to me: When one rules justly over men, ruling in the fear of God ....

Isaiah 40:13 reads, *"Who has measured the Spirit of the LORD or what man shows him his counsel?"* We notice "LORD" in the phrase "Spirit of the LORD" clearly identifying the Holy Spirit with God.

THE NEW TESTAMENT

There is much more, but now we turn to the New Testament, first to the third chapter of the Gospel of John.

A leader of the Jewish people named Nicodemus approaches Jesus at night, presumably to speak with Him in private. He says he knows Jesus is from God because of the miracles Jesus performs. Jesus, however, redirects the conversation by saying, *"unless one is born again he cannot see the kingdom of God."* Of course, the elder statesman does not understand how a person can be reborn. Jesus replies, *"Unless one is born of water and the Spirit, he cannot enter the kingdom of God."* To be born of the flesh is one thing, but to be born of the Spirit is quite another. And we must be clear: Jesus was not talking about any angel much less one named Gabriel. Only God brings life, both physical and spiritual.

The Holy Spirit works the new birth or conversion. This is clear in the passage in John 3, and we find the same in Acts 8:14–20. Also in Acts 3:1–4, the Holy Spirit is directly referred to as God. The writer of Hebrews also declares that the Holy Spirit is eternal when in reference to the power of the shed blood of Jesus:

"How much more will the blood of Christ, who through the eternal Spirit offered himself without blemish to God, purify our conscience from dead works to serve the living God" (Hebrews 9:14).

Looking back to the birth passages in Luke's Gospel, we find an answer to Mary's question to the angel Gabriel as to how she will have a baby when Gabriel says, *"The Holy Spirit will come upon you"* (Luke 1:35). It is obvious that the angel Gabriel separates himself from the Holy Spirit. Certainly, the Holy Spirit and Gabriel are not the same at all.

Clearly, neither the Qur'an nor the Bible anywhere identify Gabriel with the Holy Spirit.

Angel or Holy Spirit?

The intended goal of Islamic scholars who claim that Gabriel is the Holy Spirit is to contaminate the Christian doctrine of the Trinity. Which is it then? Is Gabriel an angel or the Holy Spirit, or maybe both at once, at least from an Islamic point of view? Our arguments above show that Gabriel is actually a jinn or demon, thus further clouding an already murky subject.

WHO IS ALLAH?

The Name "Allah"

"Allah" was the name used by Christians and Jews in the Arabian Peninsula for centuries before the Islamic era. Indeed, the word Allah was used by Jews in the Arabian Peninsula for the God of Abraham, Isaac, and Jacob before the Christian era.

To put it another way: Neither Muhammad, Abu Bakr, Umar, nor Uthman invented the word Allah. They would have known the word Allah from childhood.

It is not the word that counts; it is the content or meaning of the word.

To the Jew of that period, Allah would be the creator, the lawgiver, and the one who led the family of the patriarchs out of Egypt and gave them the Promised Land, the land of Canaan.

To the Christian of that period, Allah would be the God and Father of the Lord Jesus Christ in addition to all that the Jewish people believed about God.

It would be only natural for Muhammad to also use the term Allah in reference to the creator God. Clearly, however, Muhammad gave new definition to who or what Allah is.

Islam's Allah

Islam claims that Allah spoke to Gabriel, who then spoke to Muhammad, who then recited the revelations that originated with Allah by way of Gabriel to other people, who at some point committed them to written form.

The narrative of the collecting of the Qur'an is fascinating. There were so many variations going about that Uthman, the third caliph after Muhammad, ordered all the renditions be gathered together in order to make a uniform document. All the other manuscripts were then burned.

But the picture of Allah in the Qur'an is interesting.

Allah is distant, speaks through an angel, loves those who love him, and hates those who do not believe in him. Allah is called the greatest of deceivers and leads astray unbelievers but might also lead astray even the best of Muslims. Though Allah repeatedly refers to himself as the most beneficent, the most merciful, the most forgiving, and so on, evidence of this is lacking or scant other than what he says of himself.

It is not unfair nor a misrepresentation to say that the God of the Qur'an is far different from the God spoken of in the Bible, both the Hebrew Bible and the New Testament, the God who loves and takes a people to be His own, His children.

Transcendence versus Immanence

One of the major differences between the Bible's God and Islam's Allah is whether he is present with his creation. What we find in the Qur'an and hadith about Allah is that he is transcendent and not immanent.

In contrast, the God of the Hebrew Bible, is transcendent but is also immanent, in that He interacts personally with His people. He walked and talked with Adam and Eve in the Garden of Eden, otherwise known as Paradise. He did so until the Fall, the moment that his single law was broken, about which we read in Genesis chapter three. The terrible consequence of that event was that God's human creation was sent east of Eden. But he never left them entirely alone; he did not abandon them completely.

God once again spoke with a human being out of a burning bush on Mt. Horeb (Mt. Sinai) in the Arabian Desert, when God appeared to Moses and told him his name, Yahweh (YHWH, known as the Tetragrammaton). When Moses later led the children of Israel through the wilderness, God commanded and directed him to supervise erection of a Tabernacle, which contained a special place within it, the Holy of Holies, where would God dwell.

This was a foreshadowing of what would come later. The prophets pointed to a time when God would arrive in person. This is what the word Immanuel means—God present. We can see this in the word itself, even if we are not Hebrew literate. The last two letters of Immanuel—"el"—is the English transliteration of the Hebrew word for God, El. Then "imman," from which we get our word immanent, means present. Simply put, God with us.

This is who Jesus is.

Is Allah a fiction?

Again, my premise is that Gabriel is indeed an angel, but a fallen angel. Muhammad was correct when he thought the being that presented itself at the cave on Mt. Hira was a jinn, which is an Arabic word meaning demon. It was only his wife, Khadija, who convinced him otherwise.

The point then is: If Gabriel is a demon, and Gabriel is reciting to Muhammad what is supposedly spoken by Allah, then just who or what is Allah?

It is clear from the Hebrew Bible and the New Testament that Satan and his demons are surely angels but fallen angels who became the enemies of God. And Satan is a god, too.

> *And even if our gospel is veiled, it is veiled only to those who are perishing. In their case the god of this world has blinded the minds of the unbelievers, to keep them from seeing the light of the gospel of the glory of Christ, who is the image of God. (2 Corinthians 4:4)*

"The god of this world," Paul says, and some chapters later in the same letter he writes of those who "veil" the gospel:

> *For such men are false apostles, deceitful workmen, disguising themselves as apostles of Christ. And no wonder, for even Satan disguises himself as an angel of light. So it is no surprise if his servants, also, disguise themselves as servants of righteousness. Their end will correspond to their deeds. (2 Cor. 11:13-15)*

(Note: An apostle is a messenger, one sent with a message.)

Is Allah a fiction? No, there is an Allah, but it is Satan in disguise who directed an underling demon to approach Muhammad while Muhammad was in a trance state and therefore open to demonic invasion.

Have I committed blasphemy and of the worst sort against the Islamic trinity? Yes, indeed I have but not out of meanness or an attempt to deceive.

To say that Allah is the chief of demons (Shayton or Satan), that Gabriel is also a demon (jinn), and therefore that Muhammad was very cleverly deceived is the only possible conclusion given the evidence and arguments above. And this is what most Christians do believe, but it is a fearful endeavor to put these ideas out into the public purview, given what we have seen of Islam in these past few decades.

WHO IS MUHAMMAD?

Is Muhammad a true prophet of God?
Was he duped into thinking he was hearing words from Allah?
Did he make the whole thing up?
Was it all a dream?
Was it a scheme to acquire power and prestige?
Is Muhammad a prophet to be trusted?
Is he to be obeyed? Is he to be believed?
Is he a false prophet?

We cannot be afraid to ask these questions. Lives, both temporal and eternal, hinge on the answers, especially for Muslims. I am aware that Muslim people are sincere seekers after God. Even the most radical among them are only pursuing what has been communicated to them from the cradle.

Muslim people, in my experience, are more "religious" than most Christians, Buddhists, Hindus, and so on. Few on earth other than Muslims desire so much to be with God in Paradise. And many will do anything to assure themselves of being there. After all, no Muslim can be sure he or she will be in paradise after death, since Allah is a great deceiver and will lead astray any he chooses. Unlike the Christian who experiences assurance of salvation, the Muslim can only hope and work hard on a daily basis to earn Allah's favor.

Some commentators doubt Muhammad even existed. I am not one of these. As to whether there were those who embellished the story, especially in the latter part of the seventh and into the eighteenth century, that is a possibility. We are aware of Gnostics in the second and third centuries who did that with Jesus, who made Him into a super hero and magician.

It is well established that Muhammad was not certain in his own mind as to the nature of the entity he encountered on Mt. Hira. At first, he thought the 'angel' was a jinn, a demon; his wife Khadija convinced him it was an angel of God.

WHAT IS THE TRUTH?

That which was revealed to Muhammad differs utterly from what we see of God in the Bible. Which account is the true one?

Islam, of course, says that the revelation to Muhammad supersedes or replaces what is found in the Bible and in several significant ways. For instance, Jesus is not God come to be with us and die on a cross for our sin. Jesus is a prophet but not of the rank of Muhammad. Jesus plays a role in the last days, but he dies and ends up being buried next to Muhammad. It is rather complex, but the Jesus (Isa) of the Qur'an is not even similar to the Jesus of Christian Scripture.

Then, God in the Qur'an is separated from humans and speaks through an angel. In the Bible, God becomes flesh and dwells among us. Also, being in Paradise/heaven in the Qur'an depends upon believing that Allah alone is God and that Muhammad is his messenger. But that is only the beginning. Heaven is earned by habitually doing good deeds, working for salvation. In the Bible forgiveness, salvation, and being assured of heaven depends upon God's gift alone.

CLOSING STATEMENT

Who is Allah? Allah is either a chief demon, perhaps Satan himself, or a fantasy figure invented by Muhammad. At minimum, Allah is not the Creator God.

Who is Gabriel? Gabriel is either a jinn, meaning a demon, or again is a fantasy figure invented by Muhammad. Gabriel is not an angel of the Lord God.

Who is Muhammad? He is a seventh century man living in Arabia who was either deceived by a demonic entity or who developed a fictional account of receiving communications from God. Muhammad is not a prophet of God; he is a false prophet.

ANOTHER CONTRADICTION WITHIN ISLAM:

There is a cascading danger for Islam in its claim that Gabriel is the Holy Spirit. Islam is supposed to be monotheistic, meaning that Allah has no partners. If Gabriel is the Holy Spirit, then Gabriel is deity as well—Allah has a partner. Add to that the doctrine held by the traditionalists in Islam who believe that the Qur'an is eternal in heaven. Another partner? Consider also the reverence shown to Muhammad. Is it so complete that he is lifted to the status of deity as well? One more partner for Allah?

Muhammad is not God and never claimed to be, despite how Muslims tend to view him, and neither is Gabriel. If Gabriel is the Holy Spirit, and the Quran is eternal alongside Allah, and if every Muslim must model his own life after the "perfect man" Muhammad, it is not a stretch to say that

Islam has a fourfold divinity: Allah, Gabriel, the Qur'an, and Muhammad.

The list of inner contradictions emanating from Islam is long, and this essay only introduces some of them. For further details, please consult *Islamic Studies: Equipping the Christian Witness to Muslims*, published by Earthen Vessel Publishing at earthenvesselmedia.com.

Essay 2

A Follower of Muhammad? A Follower of Jesus?

Average Muslims are caught in a very difficult predicament—they must be followers of Muhammad and attempt to do what he did in his lifetime, if they have any chance of entering paradise. A Muslim is required to live out a very rigorous commitment to the principles and practices of Islam.

The question, "What did Muhammad do during his lifetime?" therefore becomes a very large issue for Muslim people. The following is only a short list of those things that Muhammad did and highlights the most commonly known aspects of his life.

» Once he began preaching Islam, he is not known to have earned a living other than through acquiring the spoils of conquest.

» He forced people to convert to Islam or die, or, become enslaved to Muslims and submit to them.

» He gained converts by force, some by persuasion.

» He had at least twelve wives, plus concubines, and married at least one girl under the age of ten and did have sexual relations with her while she was under ten.

» He wore a beard.

» He ate only with his right hand.

» He slept only upon his right side.

To be a true follower of Muhammad and live like he did—not easily imitated. How might a faithful Muslim then live?

To be a follower of Muhammad you would:

» Live off a welfare system. This is extremely common in Europe, for example, where those Muslims on welfare are, comparatively speaking, a very high percentage of the Muslim population. After all, how can a faithful Muslim be employed with the requirement to pray five times a day, and three of the prayers coming during normal business hours?

» View others who were not Muslims as infidels and who may then be treated in any manner necessary to secure their submission including murdering them whether man, woman, or child.

» Use force of whatever kind necessary to secure the advancement of the religion. (Every day in our newspapers this fact is highlighted and the television news broad¬casts are choked with the gory details most every evening.)

» Satisfy your sexual needs as Muhammad did by having many wives, including children.

Note: Child brides are a staple in countries where Islam predominates. Very recently, in Gaza, the terrorist organization Hamas put on a large wedding celebration for 450 couples and the brides were all little girls under ten years of age. It must be pointed out that the usual cover-ups were made to a credulous Western population that such horrific behavior is only a cultural means of providing for poor families or suggesting there is no sex until at least puberty—none of which is close to the truth. No, it is pedophilia, which is sanctioned by the Muslim culture. There are estimates that there are 51 million child brides now living on the planet and almost all are in Muslim countries. Pedophilia was not only practiced by Muhammad but is also sanctioned by the Qur'an (see Surah 65:4).

The most famous Muslim cleric of the 20th Century, Ayatollah Khomeini, said that a man can have sexual pleasure from a child as young as a baby. However, the holy man said, he should not penetrate a female; rather, sodomizing a male child was permitted. The revered ayatollah further announced that a father who gives his child for such pleasure would earn a permanent place in paradise.

Yes, this is horrific, and I will stop here with descriptions. The Ayatollah wrote a book about his views on sex with infants, animals, and more. Here is the title of the book: Ayatollah Khomeini's Book on Sex: For Shias, by LagoShia. The Ayatollah is the leading scholar and jurist for Shi'a Islam and therefore his word is law. A Wikipedia search on the subject will yield all one needs to know.

A Follower of Jesus?

Make a comparison between Jesus and Muhammad. Read one of the gospels for yourself and you will find the difference to be as different as darkness is from light, as hate is from love, and death is from life.

The Muslim, especially if born in countries with a Muslim majority, is trapped into something he or she is virtually unable to escape from. They are caught in a religious culture that, I am convinced, they would renounce if they could.

Closing Comment

Behind and beneath and within Islam lurks that which is evil. Wish it were not so, wish that Islam was actually simply another of the world's great religions as it is so often portrayed.

Why is it that mostly only Biblically-oriented Christians understand the real nature of the religion? is a question to be pondered. It would seem that all the people of the earth would be alarmed at the core teachings and practices of Islam. And it is this fact that leads me to the conclusion that there is a hideous evil strength that runs through all of that which is claimed to be a religion and which demands proper respect and acceptance.

Essay 3

Were the Crusaders and Inquisitors Christians?
Yes, No, Maybe

PART ONE: THE CRUSADERS

"Crusader" is a negative word to many, and maybe deservedly so, but we may have to reconsider the negative position. Following is a summary and examination of the history of the crusades themselves.

There were eight crusades in all, from 1095 to 1294. Oddly enough, no Arab tribes played much of a role, if any, in fighting the crusaders. This is not to say that Muslim armies were not involved, but exactly who within Islam participated is another issue.

The French initiated the **first crusade** led by Godfrey of Bouillon. The purpose was to wrest control of Jerusalem away from the Muslim Seljuk Turks, who had taken it in 1070. Jerusalem had previously been part of the Fatimid Empire, composed mostly of Shi'a Berbers from North Africa, and during their control of the Holy City, Christians were allowed to visit their special religious sites. But such was not the case with the Seljuks, who violently persecuted the Christians and desecrated and destroyed churches. After a time, Pope Urban II called for the rescue of the Holy City from the Islamic infidels.

Bouillon, certainly a member of the Roman Catholic Church, managed to murder 70,000 Muslims and even burned down synagogues crowded with Jewish people hoping to escape the violence around them. Despite the slaughter, many of the European soldiers married local Muslim and Jewish women; they settled down, and for at least forty years, the Christians and Muslims lived peacefully side-by-side. The fact remains, however, that Crusaders slaughtered a host of people.

The **second crusade** in 1144 was undertaken when a Kurdish army from Mosul (now in the modern state of Iraq) attacked a Christian fortress in Edessa (now in the modern state of Turkey). As a result, Pope Eugenius III called for a crusade. Two Christian armies, one French, the other German, were completely decimated by the Seljuk armies while on their way to join the battle at Edessa. A monk named Bernard of Clairvoux was engaged in this one. Following the crusade nearly forty more years of peace ensued.

The **third crusade** was called in 1189 by the Holy Roman Emperor Frederick Barbarossa after the army of Saladin (1137–1193), the famous Kurd who became the Sultan of Egypt, defeated the crusader army on July 4, 1187, at the Horns of Hittin, a site just above the Sea of Galilee. It proved to be the most famous of all the battles during the crusade period. Jerusalem surrendered, and Saladin dealt humanely with the survivors; there was no sacking or murdering, and the city was kept open to Christian pilgrims. But Jerusalem's fall inspired Barbarossa to lead a French army into Turkey, where he died crossing a creek. The Seljuks quickly destroyed his army.

There was, however, more to the third crusade. King Richard the Third of England (the "Lion Heart") gathered an army of Norman Knights, set off for the Holy Land, and proceeded to capture Acre and Jaffa on the Mediterranean Coast, even defeating Saladin at the battle of Arsuf.

The two commanders treated each other with respect and signed a peace treaty on September 2, 1192, the terms of which left Jerusalem in the hands of the Muslims, while the Christians retained the coastal areas where Acre, Caesarea, and Jaffa are located.

Pope Innocent III in and around 1195 called the **fourth crusade**. This one had nothing to do with the Holy Land or Muslims, but the goal was to liberate Jerusalem. The French crusaders entered Constantinople, home of the Greek Orthodox Church, who resented the presence of the Roman Catholics and rose up against the crusaders. In the battle that resulted, the crusader "Western" Christians did not kill many Greek "Eastern" Christians, but they did completely pillage the city. After a short period, the crusaders made off with their loot and headed for home. Nothing was accomplished.

Pope Honorius III, Innocent's successor, could not accept the results of the fourth crusade and called for a **fifth crusade**. This time mainly Germans and Hungarians marched off to Jerusalem by way of Egypt in 1217. The army spent three years in skirmishes with the Kurdish Ayyubids in Egypt. They failed to make headway and finally called it quits and sailed home.

The **sixth crusade's** outstanding personality was the Holy Roman Emperor Frederick II, who was the grandson of the famous Barbarossa. Frederick II's daughter was married to John of Brienne, who now ruled Jerusalem. Thinking that marriage gave him authority over Jerusalem, he called for the sixth crusade in 1225. Due to the knowledge and negotiating skills of the remarkable Frederick, the crusade was peacefully conducted without one battle or casualty.

Frederick had studied a great deal about Islamic literature, science, and philosophy, which gave him a solid platform for interaction with the leader of the Islamic army, Malik al-Kamil, who was the nephew of the great Saladin. The two leaders resolved the confrontation by signing a ten-year treaty in 1229. (Ten years was the maximum time allowed for a treaty according to Sharia Law.) Christians and Muslims alike welcomed the terms of the treaty. Unhappily, the new pope, Pope Gregory IX, hated Frederick and refused to ratify the treaty, denouncing it vigorously.

Things went from bad to worse after Sultan Kamil's death in 1238, when a maverick Turk from Russia named Baibars led a Mameluk (Muslim) army against Jerusalem, sacking it and slaughtering the citizens in 1244.

King Louis IX of France called the **seventh crusade**. In 1250 King Louis brought an army to Egypt and sailed up the Nile to Cairo, where Baibars demolished that army. Baibars warred against everyone, Christian and Muslim alike, in an effort to establish his power and authority. His hate and murderous anger were mostly directed toward Christians, and he attacked one city after the other along the Mediterranean coast—Caesarea, Safad, Jaffa, and Antioch. He killed and enslaved thousands of Christians. Jerusalem was now firmly in the hands of Muslims, and the seventh crusade came to an end.

The **eighth crusade** flowed out of the outrage perpetrated against Christians in the seventh crusade. Louis IX demanded a new crusade in the year 1270. His plan was to come through Tunis on the way to Egypt, but a few days after landing in Tunis he died of dysentery.

Baibars died in 1277 (these crusades could last for years), and his successor, Sultan Khalil, managed to finally defeat the crusaders at Acre in 1291, killing or enslaving some 60,000 Christians there.

Impact of the Crusades

The crusades deepened the divide between the Eastern and Western wings of the Catholic Church, a rift that was already well underway centuries earlier.

Related to that, the crusades greatly weakened the Byzantine Empire, which succeeded the Holy Roman Empire.

The crusades also permanently embittered relations between Christians and Muslims, and they are used to this day to rationalize a continuing hatred that often erupts into violence. The fact that both Christians and Muslims committed horrible atrocities is often forgotten or conveniently submerged. Muslims have cited Christian crusader actions as justification for their own brutality. This is not a surmise, but openly declared by contemporary Islamic jihadists, whose portfolio of rallying cries includes something close to, "Remember the crusades." They legitimize their call for revenge by pointing to what the Christians did in the crusades. This is, of course, completely disingenuous but nevertheless effective.

Promotion of religion by force of arms demonstrates the weakness of Muslim ideals, ethics, and message. To spread the faith by means of intimidation is the worst possible program, one that no one can respect. Not only the Muslims but also Christians have been guilty here. (This topic will be explored in greater detail in the second section of this essay, "The Inquisitors.")

As early as the fifth century, and many say long before, becoming a Christian required baptism by an ordained priest of the one Catholic and Apostolic Church. Faith and grace now abandoned, the Church became a power structure and fell into the same tactics employed by many other secular institutions. Some use the word "Christendom" to describe the Church as empire, combining religion with the state.

The crusades marked a departure from the Church's mission to preach the Gospel to all nations. By picking up the sword, it was giving in to the barbaric culture of that day. The Church was intertwined with the state, the state using the Church and the Church using the state to advance goals and consolidate power.

As a result, the core doctrine of conversion was severely compromised. To coerce a person into leaving one faith for another is absolutely unbiblical. Requiring a choice of whether to convert, die, or pay the tax is not exactly proper evangelism, but the Church was guilty of this just as were the Muslims, and contemporary Muslims still employ these means. It cannot be said today that the Christian Church advances by means of force and fear. (Note: Instances of wrongly motivated attempts to convert so-called "primitive" people groups were occurring well into the nineteenth century, e.g., the forcing of Western/Christian culture and religion on Native Americans on reservations and similar activities by British missionaries in India. Broadening the argument to include these examples or others is not possible in the space allowed, but we acknowledge needing to discuss this elsewhere.)

The same mentality that was seen in the crusades also resulted in the persecution of those we today call evangelical Christians, especially those who reject infant baptism, transubstantiation (Jesus being actually present in the Bread and the Cup), and the necessity of receiving other sacraments in order to go to heaven—in other words, those who adhere to salvation by grace alone, faith alone, and Christ alone.

***

The story of two ancestors of mine might be of interest now. The first concerns Sir John Philpott.

John Philpott was a "Salter and Pepperer" (a grocer) who lived in the latter part of the fourteenth century in London, England, while the One Hundred Years War with France was underway. He relied on his merchant fleet to bring foodstuffs into England from the Continent, but a combination of a weak English king and an aggressive French king meant Philpott's business was faltering. He was able, however, to convince the English king to allow him to outfit his ships into a navy and be crewed by convicts from London's prisons, of which there were plenty. The result was a series of victories by Philpott's navy, and on the strength of that he was elected Lord Mayor of London in 1388 and 1389. He was a faithful Christian, and in his will, he left 100 pounds to be distributed amongst the poor of London at Christmas time each year. In the old city of London there is still Philpott Lane where a plaque commemorating this faithful Catholic and Christian man has been installed.

Then there was another Englishman, again named John Philpott, this time living in the sixteenth century. He was a Puritan, meaning he hoped that the newly founded Church of England that broke away from the Roman Church, precipitated by King Henry VIII, would be purified—that is, would conform more closely to what we see of the church in the New

Testament. Philpott was forced into the Court of the Inquisitors and found guilty. Refusing to recant, he was burned at the stake in 1555. (Burning at the stake was a desirable form of execution, because it was thought the destruction of the body made resurrection impossible.)

PART TWO: THE INQUISITION

Although the story of the development of the Church in the centuries leading up to the "Dark Ages" (stretching from approximately AD 500 to 1500) is not so easy to uncover, there is evidence that the faith of Jesus and the early disciples was not extinguished. That it was diverted, perverted, and undermined, especially toward the end of the third century, is plain history, at least as evangelicals read it.

During that dark time, the vibrant faith we see in the New Testament gradually shifted to a more formalized, mechanical, ritualistic, even magical understanding of what it meant to be a follower of Jesus. Especially after the so-called conversion of Constantine in the early fourth century, people became members of the Church and were counted among the faithful, despite their never hearing the real Gospel message or knowing much of anything about the core doctrines of Scripture.

The power of the Church over salvation, the only really important issue in life, was under the control of an ecclesiastical hierarchy. Those who rebelled against this were the targets of the Inquisition, the first court of which was formed around the year 1231 and continued for some three or four centuries. From the Church's point of view, the Inquisition was necessary, because many good Catholics were turning away from the doctrines of the Church, especially after publication of the Bible in common languages, which allowed people to see what the Bible actually taught. For nearly a thousand years it had been hidden in a dark covering of non-intelligible Latin, Greek, or Hebrew.

The renaissance of Biblical understanding forced the established Church to react, and energetically; heresy became the most heinous of all crimes. There is evidence that many were troubled by the means used to keep the Church pure. Ecclesiastical leaders would often plead with secular authorities for sentences to be carried out mercifully. In the early days of the persecution, Roman Church officials acted ruthlessly. For instance, the Cathari (or Albigenses) and the Waldenses were persecuted, sometimes to death, during the 1220s by the order of Pope Gregory IX.

Were the Crusaders and Inquisitors Christians? 33

Fringe Christian groups were not the only ones to be sought out by the Inquisitors. As with John Philpott in 1555, the point at the center of the trials had to do with the elements of the Mass, otherwise known as Communion, Eucharist, or the Lord's Supper. Along with the Reformers (i.e., Martin Luther and John Calvin), Philpott believed the bread of the Eucharist was just bread and the juice in the cup just juice. But the Church had developed the concept that the bread was transformed by an act of the priest into the actual body, the flesh, of Jesus. Likewise, the juice invisibly, magically, became the actual blood of Jesus.

Two Latin words were pronounced by the priest before the Mass began—*hocus pocus*—and when the words were pronounced, the magical power inherited from Peter and passed down through the properly ordained priesthood transformed the substances, shazam!

How this came to be is not possible to describe here, but there is an actual history to it. The short version is this: The Church had become far too Western in its understanding of the Middle Eastern document we call the Bible, both Old and New Testaments. And when Jesus said, "Truly, truly, I say to you, unless you eat the flesh of the Son of Man and drink his blood, you have no life in you. Whoever feeds on my flesh and drinks my blood has eternal life, and I will raise him up on the last day. For my flesh is true food, and my blood is true drink" (John 6:53-55), the Roman Church took His words literally.

To take Jesus' words literally, however, would have been ludicrous for a Jewish person in the first century. And the early history of the Church clearly reveals that the passage was taken metaphorically—after all, the Church was composed mostly of Jews for the first generation. The point was that the disciples were to trust in and believe in Jesus as the Savior and that His death on the cross, with His broken body and shed blood, was the once-forever sacrifice for sin. Therefore, long after the "Eastern" sense of things was lost, the "Western" mindset misunderstood much of the nature and means of salvation.

The Inquisition was aimed at Christians, but Muslims and Jews were also tried, and many were executed. It is only natural that Muslims and Jews would have a negative reaction to this, and it is certainly possible that it yet lingers as something else horrible that Christendom perpetrated and thus could be avenged in whatever era.

During the period of the Inquisition there were undoubtedly thousands of bishops, priests, and regular members of the Roman Church who sincerely thought they were being faithful Christians to support and participate in what they perceived as a cleansing of their Church from heretical doctrine and practice. Undoubtedly, there were thousands of Christians who were horrified at what was being done in the name of Jesus Christ. And during the period of history when the Church and state were wed, significant resistance was virtually out of the question. Such resistance finally came in 1517 under the inspiration of a Catholic monk named Martin Luther.

PART THREE: YES, NO, MAYBE

Were those who conducted the Inquisition real Christians?
Were the crusaders real Christians?
Were the Muslims who fought against the crusaders real Muslims? Or, to put it another way, are those Muslims who engage in violent jihad today the real Muslims?
To these questions the answers are, Yes, No, and Maybe.

LOOKING AT CHRISTIANS

It must be said that no one could possibly know for sure whether real and actual born-again Christians committed atrocities against Muslims and Jews, in that day or in this. If a group of careful observers had watched the murder of Muslims and Jews at the hands of people known as Christians during the crusades and at other times, would they have known for certain which was the right conclusion? The proper answer would have to be, No!

Why is this so? The core of the answer lies in the mystery of conversion. While one can be baptized, join a church, and even reform his or her life, this is far from genuine Christian conversion. Being a part of a church does not mean one is a Christian. Conversion means that the Holy Spirit indwells the one believing in Jesus, the one who has had all sin removed and forgiven. It is a profound spiritual experience not an intellectual or emotional one. It is something God does completely apart from anything an individual can do. It is miracle and mystery. Every pastor who has ministered to a congregation for ten or more years knows that in that congregation are those who have truly been born again and those who have not.

Not that every real Christian does right and lives right. The Christian life is a growing up into the fullness of Christ, little by little—first as an

Were the Crusaders and Inquisitors Christians?

infant, then a toddler, young child, older child, adolescent, teenager, young adult, adult, older adult, and senior. Still after a lifetime of maturing, the Christian is not anywhere perfect until in heaven and in the presence of our holy God.

Is it possible that a Christian could be deceived into thinking that killing and persecuting others because they believed differently is justified? Yes, it is possible.

Might Christians commit horrific acts because they were told to do so by powerful religious authorities? Maybe. Might Muslims? Maybe.

Would a Biblically literate Christian believe he or she was serving God by persecuting or even killing "infidels"? No, unless there was some unknown source of intimidation going on behind the scenes and/or such Christian had his or her mind bent to the point that they became merely tools of evil.

Perhaps the right answer for all of these questions is, Maybe!

Would persecuting or killing a non-Christian win approval with God? Would it ensure a place in heaven? To both, the answer is an unequivocal, No!

Would defending the cause of Christianity, the Church, a Christian leader, or anything else in all creation by harming others merit the favor of God? Certainly not! Would dying in defense of the God of Scripture assure a place in paradise? In no way!

This is my solemn opinion as a follower of Jesus.

Essay 4

Looking at Muslims

A growing number of Christians and non-Christians alike declare that what is observed in the Islamic State (ISIS, also called *Daesh* from an Arabic acronym) and other groups that engage in violent jihad does not represent true Islam. This, however, is debatable.

Muhammad did force non-Muslims into submission and made them pay a tax to stay alive. Muhammad did behead captured enemies, or at least ordered such and then observed the process. He did cut off the hands of thieves. He did arrange that captured women and children be sold as slaves. He did permit captured women to be taken as concubines; in fact, his last wife was a beauty he had rescued from a Jewish tribe that the Muslim army had defeated. Muhammad authorized lying whenever the cause of Islam was being defended or advanced. He did practice forced conversions. Whatever Muhammad did in his lifetime, as spelled out in the Qur'an, found in the hadith, or seen in the biography of Muhammad (called the Sira, written by Ibn Ishaq), are being imitated by the Islamic State now. And this Caliphate does not deny but proudly embraces this fact.

Not only do they not deny they are imitating Muhammad's tactics, but IS would view non-compliance to be at minimum weakness bordering on apostasy. This is the present situation. Muhammad taught that Islam should be global and that Shar'ia Law be universal, which would result in the entire world then being at peace. It is the task of Muslims to bring this about. Anything less than this is un-Islamic.

Then there is Salafism. This term describes Muslims who practice a conservative, even radical form of their faith. They attempt to imitate Muhammad and hope to live under Shar'ia Law. It is just that they cannot do so except in a place where it is politically and culturally possible. "Most

Salafis are not jihadists, and most adhere to sects that reject the Islamic State," writes Graeme Wood in his March 2015 article in *Atlantic* entitled, "What ISIS Really Wants." They might, however, if given the chance, be every bit as strict as violent jihadists. Wood states that Salafis might implement "monstrous practices such as slavery and amputation – but at some future point." The Salafis' stated agenda is to purify their personal lives, including personal hygiene, and to be faithful in prayer and observance of all standard forms of the main rituals of Islam.[1]

Are all those who promote and/or engage in violent jihad real Muslims? If the answer is No, then it must be asked, "How could this be?"

There are many reasons why one would turn to violent jihad other than wanting to live like Muhammad. Is it possible that young men and women living in very poor circumstances, without much of a future, could be recruited into something they would later regret? Perhaps peer pressure overcomes them. Perhaps boredom, hopelessness, or a strong sense of inferiority might trigger the desire for a radical change in living. By means of the Internet, which jihadists use but detest at the same time, they recruit these vulnerable youth.

Not only those who grow up in less-than-ideal circumstances are attracted to violence and murder. It is enough that Muhammad both sanctioned and participated in such. The desire for a wonderful eternal future is a powerful magnet and may be the strongest motivator for a violent defense or advance of Islam.

The Internet also shows clearly what is available in the Western world; could envy be an instigating element that plays on the Muslim mind? Or, might a motivation be a chance for a quick ticket to paradise and seventy-two virgins, which may appear to be the only way to get love? Might young men and women be driven to distraction, to a cultic or toxic state of mind and made willing to do almost anything to lift themselves out of

---

1   By "Personal hygiene" is meant the intent to properly observe and avoid the many ways that Muslims might defile themselves before prayer. A chief instance of this is to avoid splashing oneself with urine in the toilet. Proper techniques for washing feet, arms, hands, and face before prayer is critical in the Muslim mind. This little section could continue for many pages describing the means of coping with and defending against the evil jinn (demons), since hygiene in the Muslim world is not what non-Muslim Westerners understand but is more concerned with superstitions about the supernatural.

depression and despair?

Since Islam is both religion and state, which predominates? Or is there such a blending that there is no religion or state, just Islam? Islam is yet very much tribally oriented, one tribe against another, which is plain to see in daily news stories. Is the Muslim fighting for Muhammad, the imam, the umma (Muslim community), the political boundary, or what? This question might receive a hundred different answers, and silence as an answer could be expected.

Are all fighters with al-Qaeda, the Taliban, the various Shia and Sunni militias, even with ISIS, true Muslims? Yes, No, and Maybe! Only God knows.

Essay 5

A Fundamental Error of Islam

When visiting a local Sunni mosque, I was given a booklet entitled *A Brief Illustrated Guide to Understanding Islam*. The anonymous author states:

Muslims believe that Jesus was not crucified. It was the plan of Jesus' enemies to crucify him, but God saved him and raised him up to Him. And the likeness of Jesus was put over another man. Jesus' enemies took this man and crucified him, thinking that he was Jesus.

The author backed up his contention with a quote from the Qur'an:

…They said: "We killed the Messiah Jesus, son of Mary, the messenger of God." They did not kill him, nor did they crucify him, but the likeness of him was put on another man (and they killed that man)…Qur'an 4:157

A fundamental error of Islam is this denying of the crucifixion of Jesus Christ while saying another man who looked like Jesus was actually placed on the cross. This is essentially a form of Gnosticism called Docetism.

Gnostics existed prior to the Christian era and were able to incorporate varying religious thought into their system. The Gnostics viewed matter as evil and mind or thought as good. The Christian incarnation, that is, God become flesh in Jesus of Nazareth, ran counter to their core doctrine. Therefore, they developed the idea that Jesus did not actually die on a cross, rather someone who looked like Jesus did. This belief system is called Docetism, based on the Greek dokeo, meaning "to seem like."

The basic principle of Docetism was refuted by the Apostle John in 1 John 4:2-3:

By this you know the Spirit of God: every spirit that confesses that

Jesus Christ has come in the flesh is from God; and every spirit that does not confess Jesus is not from God; and this is the spirit of the antichrist, of which you have heard that it is coming, and now it is already in the world.

Also, 2 John 7:
For many deceivers have gone out into the world, those who do not acknowledge Jesus Christ as coming in the flesh. This is the deceiver and the antichrist.

Ignatius of Antioch (AD 98–117), Irenaeus (115–190), and Hippolatus (170-235) wrote against the Gnostic error in the early part of the second century.

Docetism was condemned at the Council of Chalcedon in 451.

Many sects and cults over the centuries have taken a Gnostic stance and thus substitute their own teaching as the means of salvation. This is precisely what Islam has done.

And Islam must do so. If salvation is based solely on Christ's death on the cross, where our sin was atoned for, then Islam has nothing to offer but is in fact a conduit for false salvation.

Islam is agonizingly focused on attaining eternity in paradise, or heaven, which is really the same thing. Heaven is fellowship with a holy God and is made possible only through the cleansing blood of Jesus shed on the cross.

Islam and Christianity are polar opposites. Both cannot be right at the same time. This reality must be squarely faced.

The purest, most religious Muslim or the filthiest, most hypocritical Christian. Which would I prefer to be?

Which am I? I am the latter, and due to the utter holiness of the Triune God, I remain the filthy, hypocritical Christian until that day I stand before the Judgment of God on the Last Day and hear my Lord say, "Well done, good and faithful servant, enter into the joy of your rest."

Essay 6

The Weakness of Islam

In nearly every edition of major American newspapers are stories of Muslims somewhere, east or west, engaged in acts of violence—in the name of Allah. Suicide bombing, kidnapping, killing Christians, Jews, and Hindus, burning churches and temples, destroying ancient religious relics, protesting free expressions of religion and the press—such terrorist reports are routine. What does this indicate about the very fabric of Islam?

I say it demonstrates a core weakness.

By weakness, I mean Islam is not able to compete in the spiritual marketplace of ideas. It must instead resort to repression, intimidation, and violence. Perhaps there is a sense of inferiority in that Muslims are gripped by the fear that Islam is not able to stand alongside Christianity, which does not seek to gain influence and converts by dependence on questionable, cultic methods.

I am reminded of Paul who, prior to his conversion, vigorously persecuted the Church. Many Bible scholars think he was motivated by a fear that his religious beliefs were inadequate or even erroneous. Paul was a terrorist while he was still known as Saul, according to the Biblical account in Acts. Yet after Jesus appeared to him on the road to Damascus, Paul no longer threw men, women, and children in prison merely because they believed in Jesus. Rather, he himself became a simple preacher of the gospel armed only with the message of a crucified and risen Savior.

Paul learned from Jesus, who taught His disciples to turn the other cheek, to pray for their enemies, and to do good to those who treated them shamefully. Jesus taught that His followers were to love their neighbors as themselves and to do to others as they would have done to them. Jesus said nothing of killing infidels or repressing religious teachings. He did warn of false prophets whose aim would be to deceive and corrupt.

Clearly, however, He did not advocate imprisoning or killing them. In one instance, Jesus taught His disciples to simply go on to the next town when opposition arose. Jesus Himself practiced this, as did Paul throughout his missionary journeys.

Consider a society like Saudi Arabia where even the simple recounting of the Christian message to a Muslim is a capital offense. That is weakness in the extreme.

Islamic evangelistic strategy, known as da'wa, is so very often fueled by intimidation and violence. "Convert or die" has too often been the Muslim message. Am I exaggerating here? I don't think so, since sufficient historical data supports my claim, both ancient and modern. In fact, I think that the Islamic means of spreading the faith are held in check only by fear of retaliation from target peoples.

Biblical Christianity has entirely different weapons of warfare. Paul wrote, *"For though we walk in the flesh, we are not waging war according to the flesh. For the weapons of our warfare are not of the flesh but have divine power to destroy strongholds"* (2 Corinthians 10:3-4). Such is the power of the message of Jesus.

Evangelical Christians proclaim the message of the Cross of Jesus and His resurrection. The Holy Spirit of God then convicts individuals of their rebellion against God and draws them to the Savior, Jesus Christ, who has completely provided for their salvation. No one can be forced to become a Christian; no one can even "join" Christianity or apply for membership. It is a work of God and not of man. One of the great weaknesses of Islam is that it arose and continues to exist as the work of man. Few voluntarily choose to join Islam, especially in recent years now that the religion was been partially unmasked. It is usually by birth and community attachments that one becomes a Muslim. And especially in Muslim-dominated countries it is nearly impossible to leave it. This again is a great weakness. There is no religious freedom for Muslims to come and go, to be faithful or not; there is only fear of the community, of hellfire, and peer pressure. To be an apostate Muslim, that is one who has declared faith in Jesus rather than Muhammad, is to be classified worse than an infidel. The result is often death.

Paul trusted in the work of the Holy Spirit and did not revert to his old ways of violence and imprisonment—fleshly warfare. In Ephesians, Chapter 6, he describes the "armor of God"—which is the belt of truth, the breastplate of righteousness, for the feet the gospel of peace, the shield of faith, the helmet of salvation, and the sword of the Spirit, which is the word of God (see Ephesians 6: 10-20).

This is strength. This is confidence. This is peace. This is actual dependence on and submission to God.

Essay 7

Islam's Cultic Connection

Islam is rarely critiqued by journalists because it can be dangerous to do so. This has been less true since September 11, 2001, because people are interested in Islam and are searching for answers.

However, it is still risky to write anything that may impugn Islam and especially the founder, Muhammad. This is one reason why I call Islam a cult. Muslims often treat opponents with something less than kindness as they seek to defend the honor of "Allah."

What Is a Cult?

My working definition of a cult is non-theological. Traditionally, Christians apply the term to Bible-based groups that have departed significantly from the mainstream and historical creeds. Such cults frequently deny the full deity and humanity of Jesus; His atoning work on the cross; His bodily resurrection; and His return at the end of the age to judge the living and the dead.

However, here I employ a secular definition of a cult: "any group that uses psychological or sociological techniques to recruit, motivate, and retain adherents."

Cults are not necessarily religious; they may be political, commercial, educational/therapeutic, or economic in nature. They may be large or small, named or unnamed, known or unknown.

Cults may have a leader or be without a leader. The common feature is the use of control mechanisms that violate the individuality of participants in the three areas stated above: recruitment, motivation, and retention.

Is Islam Cultic?

Many would deny that Islam has the characteristics of a cult. But why is Islam not a cult when in many Muslim-dominated countries it is a capital offense to hand Muslims a Bible or explain Christianity (or any other religion) to them?

Saudi Arabia, the guardian of Islam's most holy shrines at Mecca and Medina, is a highly restricted society where Christians are not allowed any public expression of their faith.

Why is Islam not a cult when it is virtually impossible for a Muslim to leave the religion, even if he merely wishes to become an atheist or agnostic?

Why is Islam not a cult when Muslim warriors force their religion on people? The history of Islam is full of that kind of "proselytization."

It is true that the Roman Catholic Church has in the past forced "pagans" to adopt Catholicism. However, that church has acknowledged that it was both wrong-headed and anti-Christian to do so and has terminated the practice.

As a Baptist, I can say that in 500 years of our history we have not engaged in such tactics and neither have any of the traditionally Evangelical, Protestant denominations.

SATANIC VERSES

A vivid illustration of the cultic nature of Islam is the case involving the novelist Salman Rushdie. Rushdie had a death contract issued against him for writing his book, The Satanic Verses and supposedly impugning the character of Muhammad. Yet novelists, journalists, commentators, filmmakers, and television producers routinely blaspheme Jesus of Christianity and the Creator God without reprisals made against them by Christians.

Of course, the fatwa against Salman Rushdie is blamed on "fundamentalists" and "extremists," exonerating most Muslims who live in Western countries as peace-loving citizens. But the loyalty inculcated by Islam runs deeper than allegiance to any nation. Muslims will change political affiliations if needed, but their commitment to the defense of Islam easily becomes fanatical.

A CONTRAST

How insecure and weak must Islam be when Muslims threaten those who oppose it with violence rather than use reasoned defense. Such paranoid behavior renders Islam resistant to self-evaluation and exposes its internal deficiencies.

Biblical Christianity thrives in a free, pluralistic, and democratic society. It neither needs nor benefits from the support of a nation state. By contrast, Islamic control in many countries is totalitarian, dictatorial, and oppressive.

In countries ruled by Sharia Law, minor infractions may be punished by the loss of a hand, a foot, or life itself. Muslim women have been stoned to death for inadvertently exposing an ankle or forearm in public. The much-touted "mercy" of Islam is hard to detect.

Disillusionment with the religion simmers under the surface in Islamic societies. Many Muslim immigrants to Western countries, if not pressured by the local Muslim community to tow the line, either moderate or abandon Islam altogether. Others go through the religious motions, but their hearts are not in it.

THE COST OF DEFECTION

Today there is a "rallying to the cause," as many Muslims believe the war against terrorism is between "Christian America" and Islam. But many Muslims would prefer to be free of such influences if they could. Of course, Muslim clerics in the West realize this and do not hesitate to isolate their constituents from non-Muslim influence. Isolation is a typical cultic mechanism—defections are treated most seriously.

In lands dominated by Islam, the rule is "once a Muslim, always a Muslim." Like the Mafia, Islam is difficult to leave, and any who defect do so at a great price. Most cults ostracize defecting people, cutting them off from family, friends, and even employment. Muslims sometimes assassinate people who leave their religion. How very cultic!

WORLD RULE

Cults are dangerous—they control and manipulate those under their sway. Islamic leaders may issue a declaration (fatwa) or call for a holy war (jihad). Muslims are expected to obey these calls despite their individual feelings. As with the fatwa against Rushdie, Muslims remained under a theoretical obligation to kill him even though restrained from doing so by the law of the land.

If Islam were not so fractured into sects and splinter movements, the non-Muslim world would face a more serious enemy than it does today. Islam sanctions the murder of infidels and, of course, I am one, and so is anyone who is not a Muslim. It is no secret that Islam's goal is world rule.

This is not some right-wing conspiracy theory; it is the stated aim of Islam.

On the other hand, while Christians seek to share the Good News of Christ worldwide, they are not intent on forcing people to accept Christianity, much less eliminating those who reject the message.

SPIRITUAL PROCESS

Conversion to Christ is a spiritual process, not the recitation of a formula such as, "There is no god but Allah and Muhammad is his prophet." Biblical Christianity is about grace, which is God's gift of faith and forgiveness.

Christianity is grounded both in the sacrifice Jesus offered for sin on the cross, and upon His resurrection that declares that those for whom He died are "justified." No one becomes a Christian on the basis of his or her works or actions. Rather, conversion is something God brings about. This is why the New Testament uses the term "new birth" to describe it (see John 3: 1-15). Humans do not control their physical birth, and with the new (spiritual) birth it is the same. Salvation is accomplished through God's power, not man's. No public or private declaration will ever make a Christian out of anyone.

REVISED RELIGION

Islam is classed with those religious groups that have "revised" Christianity. Some of these are The Church of Latter Day Saints (Mormons) and Jehovah's Witnesses.

In these groups, including Islam, Jesus is acknowledged and honored as a prophet. He may even be worshipped to some degree. Yet Jesus' teachings are declared to be incomplete and outdated. They must therefore be replaced or superseded by the teachings of _____ (insert name of group or prophet).

The Christianity Muhammad knew in the sixth and seventh centuries in the Arabian Peninsula was far different from New Testament Christianity—which had radically deteriorated. Observing the deficiencies in Judaism and a degenerate Christianity, Muhammad replaced them with his own concepts. This is understandable. The result, however, is not an improvement; it is simply another failed revisionist effort.

DOWNGRADE

It is patronizing, too, for Islam to say it respects Jesus as a prophet while denying or altering what He said about himself and what the New Testament writers said concerning Him. I am thinking of such Scriptures as John 1:1-3 and Colossians 1:15-20 among many others. Of course, the Mormons and Jehovah's Witnesses do the same. Revisionist cults must downgrade Jesus so that the "new, improved prophet" (or "truth") can be presented as a replacement.

If Jesus is God in the flesh—Emmanuel, as the Christian Scripture proclaims; and if Jesus is the Messiah prophesied by the great Hebrew prophets; and if Jesus is the only Lord and Savior who will return to judge the living and the dead, then it is impossible to replace him.

Revelation and Misunderstanding

The Qur'an declares that the Bible, both Old and New Testaments, is a revelation from God. But it then proceeds to reject the clear message of the Bible! If the Bible is accurate about Jesus, there is no need for the Qur'an or Muhammad.

So, was Muhammad using flattery or attempting to patronize Christians when he seemed to honor Jesus? Or did he simply not understand? Essentially, Muhammad rejected a Christianity vastly different from the teaching of the New Testament.

Another sign of a cult is the way it keeps its adherents in the dark about other faiths. I doubt whether Muslims today know much about the message of Jesus and His Gospel. They know only what they have been told by their religious teachers. How accurate would we expect this information to be considering that the Qur'an is their authority?

To make it even worse, there is a general misunderstanding of what Christianity is. One misconception, for example, is that the West is Christian and that America is a Christian nation. Obviously, all that goes by the name of Christian is not Christian. To grasp what is the true essence of Jesus' teachings, we must examine the primary source, the Bible.

Christians reject the belief that Muhammad is the prophet of God. Christians reject the Qur'an as a revelation from God. At least this is an honest position, innocent of any effort to mislead, flatter, confuse, or patronize.

What about the Crusades?

Muslims often ask, "What about the Crusades?" The intention of this question is often to deflect attention from the violence and oppression displayed by Muslims worldwide in the name of Allah.

Yes, there were the Crusades, and historians debate the complex tangle of religion and politics that gave rise to them. The Church of that era did not always pursue a true Christian and Biblical agenda. And this same authoritarian organization persecuted Jews and Protestants also. This same medieval church persecuted to the death those who believed the truths that I, as a Christian today, hold precious.

Is it therefore accurate for Muslims to blame all that goes by the name Christian for the Crusades? Would it not be fairer and wiser to discriminate amongst Christians? After all, most people do not blame all Muslims for the actions of some extremists.

Women in Islam

Another cultic aspect of Islam is the oppression of women in countries under Islamic rule. It is shocking, deviant, and evil.

Why is this frightful treatment tolerated? Why is there such an exaggerated fear and mistrust of women? Islamic spokesmen say the women are merely being protected. The women themselves generally resent their treatment and lowly status, but are seemingly powerless to bring about change.

The plight of young men and women in Islamic countries is sad indeed. Their isolation from one another distorts normal social relationships between the sexes. Wealthy (and usually older) men can have four wives and as many concubines as they can afford, while younger, poorer men, are deprived. This deplorable situation stems directly from the nature and traditions of Islam itself as well as the tribal culture from which it sprang.

Women are denied education in countries ruled by strict Sharia law. Why? Is it to keep women in their place? Why must women cover themselves so that not even an ankle can be seen in public? These are twisted gender mores.

Moderate Muslims claim that these practices are only enforced by extremists. The "extremists" claim they are only interpreting Islam in the purest manner possible! Who is right?

Fruit of Islam

Islamic political control has prevented social progress and economic development. For example, does anyone own a car made in an Islamic country?

How about a television set, a computer, an alarm clock, an airplane, or a boat? Why are many Islamic countries among the poorest in the world even while their oil reserves are vast?

Where do wealthy Muslims send their young people to be educated? To Western countries, for the most part, since those countries freely entertain examination of all points of view for the widest number of topics using the latest discoveries and thinking.

The cultic nature of Islam prevents Muslim-dominated countries from developing middle class wealth, which would require an ever-increasing importation of Western ways, and this is feared and condemned by Muslim clerics. The shot callers in Islam fear the rise of a middle class.

Muslims have undoubtedly contributed to the world's storehouse of achievements. But if we look at the Islamic nations today, we see they are something less than wonderful. Except for Afghan refugees trying to enter Pakistan, I haven't read about people lining up at their borders waiting to get in. Islam is sometimes described as the "beautiful religion," but where can this beauty be seen? What Islamic country practices Islam in such a way that someone might be motivated to move there?

It is one thing for Muslim leaders to disown the September 11 terrorists as extremists. It is another to demonstrate peaceful moderation and tolerance.

Please understand I am not saying that Muslim people are not as capable, intelligent, and worthy as any other people. Rather, it is the toxic and repressive nature of recruitment, retention, and motivation that is cultic.

Muslims are born into a religious heritage they did not choose and cannot walk away from. They are molded by their environment into dedicated Muslims; there is essentially no choice available for them—they are stuck.

The Major Difference

Islam is a religion based on performance, whereas Biblical Christianity is grounded on God's grace. The Islamic deity rewards obedience. Muslim heaven, or paradise, must be earned, either by martyrdom or by carefully keeping rules and regulations.

And since Allah is depicted as remote and detached from the individual Muslim, there is no assurance of salvation nor any confidence that even the faithful Muslim will achieve paradise.

Works-based religion can and does inspire fear and extremism in those who take it seriously. It is not surprising that some go to extremes to curry the favor of the deity and their religious leaders, especially when a favorable eternity is at stake.

The Qur'an assures martyrs that they will attain paradise, and it is this very promise that attracts and motivates suicide bombers, including those who turned commercial airliners into missiles on September 11. Since that day, the Qur'anic command to "strike terror into the heart" of the infidel has been obeyed more and more often by young men and women recruited by watching on the Internet horrific violence against innocent civilians in dozens of filmed executions and other gruesome attacks.

Biblical Christianity, on the other hand, emphasizes grace, which signifies "God's giving". Through Jesus Christ, God imparts forgiveness and salvation as a free gift, apart from any good work. Salvation is by grace, not by works (Ephesians 2:4-10). Even extreme devotion, sacrifice, and obedience will never secure God's favor.

Furthermore, Christians have assurance of salvation by the inner witness of the Holy Spirit, so they are not left in doubt and insecurity (Romans 8:15-17). Everlasting life with God in heaven is given to the Christian through the work of God the Son. It cannot be lost, since God the Father keeps the believer by His great power (John 10:27-30).

AN ABSURDITY

Cults employ mind-bending techniques to induce their followers to be obedient—this has long been understood.

What about the mind-boggling promise of seventy-two virgins available for the pleasures of every martyred Islamic warrior? This is as extreme an example as can be found even in the strangest cult sects!

Certainly, for poor, young, love-starved men, whose future is clouded at best, the promise of unlimited fleshly pleasure in the hereafter might be an inducement to die for the sake of Allah. But is this obscene and sexist doctrine true? Moderate Islamic interpreters say no; the sexually oriented promises are unfounded. Yet, this perverse promise is constantly embraced. Many a mind-bent warrior has killed and died to acquire his virgins.

A Challenge

Harassment of Muslims is unacceptable, and this essay is not an attempt to bring grief to Muslim people.

However, I would challenge Muslims to examine their religion—indeed, their hearts and minds, and ask themselves these questions:

Why am I a Muslim? Is my commitment to Islam based on a free decision apart from family influences?

What is my attitude towards those of other religions, particularly Jews and Christians?

Are my attitudes cultic in any way?

Do I honestly think that killing Jews and Christians serves Allah?

Do I believe it is a Muslim's duty to defend Islam by martyrdom or suicide?

Should I support religious tolerance for people of other faiths in Muslim-dominated countries like Saudi Arabia?

Many Muslims are seekers after God, and this is good. The Hebrew prophet Jeremiah wrote: "You will seek me and find me; when you seek me with all your heart" (Jeremiah 29:13).

Whether Muslim, Hindu, Buddhist, Jew, nominal Christian, or nothing at all—the challenge is to seek God because He can be found. Jesus said, *"Seek first his kingdom and his righteousness, and all these things shall be yours as well"* (Matthew 6:33).

Knowing God

Regardless of our religious background, we are created in the image of God. We have been made by and for Him, and we will never be satisfied until we know Him personally. The Creator God sent His Son, Jesus, to break down the walls of separation between men and reconcile all kinds of people to Himself (Ephesians 2:14-18).

The challenge is to make up your own mind about Jesus Christ. Learn about Him yourself and do not merely accept the opinions of others.

Find a New Testament, read the story of His life, and see if you find anything amiss with Him. Is there any sin, or anything false, in the one who came from God? Find an Old Testament and read the prophecies of the Messiah (which is Hebrew for "Christ"), passages like Psalm 22 and Isaiah 53. Are these passages not about Jesus?

If you seek Him, He will be found.

Essay 8

My First Essay on Islam

I am sixty years old, born in Portland, Oregon, and now live in Mill Valley, California. I became a Christian at age twenty-one. I am married with five children and eight grandchildren. I was ordained in 1966; most of the time my denomination has been Baptist.

The first spiritual truth I knew was that I was a lost and hopeless sinner. This is while I was in the military. My life was ordinary, no crises, but after hearing the message of Jesus and the cross, I understood for the first time that He died in my place, taking my sin upon Himself. The second truth I learned was that Jesus is the Savior, raised from the dead, who loves me and would give me the gift of eternal life.

I have been in the ministry ever since my ordination, most of that as a pastor, and have seen many hundreds become followers of Jesus. For Christians this means conversion, or the new birth, one and the same thing. We are not born Christian, though we might be born into a culture heavily influenced by Christianity. But this can be problematic since we can mistakenly believe that we are Christian due to our physical birth.

Now, as to the issue of Christianity, Islam, and Judaism worshipping the same God—yes and no. Certainly Judaism and Christianity see the God of Abraham, Isaac, and Jacob as the Creator God. Islam, however, worships Allah, and Allah was a local deity worshipped by people of a particular area, the area where Mohammed lived.

Mohammed was born in Arabia and lived in Mecca. He belonged to the Quraysh tribe that controlled the worship at the Ka'bah shrine, which contains the "black stone." This shrine was the center of idol worship with more than 360 idols being honored. The Arabic word for idol is "ilah" and "al" is Arabic for god. Allah, a combination of these two, and was the name for the primary god worshipped in Mecca. In addition, Allah was the name pre-Islamic Arabs used for the moon god, which was represented by the crescent moon. This symbol, the crescent moon, was used for many idols in pre-Islamic Arabia. Indeed, it was common among pre-Islamic Arabs to pray facing Mecca and to observe a fast one month a year. Mohammed incorporated many pre-Islamic religious concepts into the Qur'an. Mohammed merely declared that only Allah would be worshipped to the exclusion of all other idols. Allah was essentially then the name of a local moon god.

The claim that Islam worships the same God as Judaism and Christianity is false. This is not to say that Muslims are not people of good will who are seeking peace. Some may and some may not. My concern is spiritual not political. If I had a merely political agenda, I might overlook the theological differences between the religions. However, the issue that transcends all others is a personal relationship with God. Error here is ultimate, the greatest of all enemies.

Now Judaism, in rejecting Jesus as Messiah and Savior, makes a mistake. To worship the Son of God, Jesus, is to worship God the Father. He who has the Son has the Father, but he who does not have the Son does not have the Father. To love one is to love the other. The Scripture is plain on this point. Many Jewish people do trust in Jesus, however. And Muslims may also trust in Jesus—anyone may. The names of the various religions are merely man-made designations. The fact is there is one God and we are all made in His image. I am not personally concerned about religious labels, but I am a follower of Jesus Christ, He is my Lord and Savior. He is not God of the Christians; He is the Lord of heaven and earth.

Many groups claim the God of the Bible as their God—groups like the Mormons, the Jehovah's Witnesses, and so on. But they reject or deny what the Bible says about the Messiah in both the Old and New Testaments. Are we Christians bound to accept the picture of Jesus that the Jehovah's Witnesses, for example, give us? They say Jesus is the archangel Michael and not Emmanuel, God with us, despite, for example, what the prophet Isaiah wrote (see Isaiah 7:14). Am I bound to accept the pronouncements of the Jehovah's Witnesses? Because groups like the Mormons say their prophet is the latest prophet superseding all others, am I bound to believe this? The Mormons say their Book of Mormon is the final truth and all that came before is good but not the final revelation of God. Do I have to believe this?

Mohammed claimed to be the final prophet and the Qur'an to be the final revelation. Am I bound to believe this? Numerous so-called prophets have come along with new versions of truth—so what! They each diminish or do a re-make on Jesus so they can insert into the place of the Lord Jesus Christ their own prophet, revelation, or holy book. No, we are wise to this in America; these prophets and angelic revelations—they are a dime a dozen.

I live in a free society that has freedom of religion. My faith is personal, and I don't care what anyone else thinks about it. I did not choose God anyway, He chose me. He called me and gave me faith in Jesus, His only begotten Son. I am not a Christian because I was born one, I did not even want to be a Christian. But when God, by His Holy Spirit, showed me that Jesus, the perfect lamb of God, had died in my place, had taken all my sin upon Himself, and through His resurrection gives me the gift of eternal life, well, that was enough for me. I did not figure anything out, I did no good religious work; no, God changed my heart, helped me repent, and gave me faith.

This is the Gospel. Please know that I wish all the people of the world would live in peace and harmony. I have no anger or resentment toward Muslims. For what it is worth, I am also the manager of a baseball team, and I just appointed as my primary coach a Muslim man. And my leadoff hitter and second baseman is also a Muslim.

Would you be a Muslim if you did not have to be? Could you walk away from Islam? What might happen if you decided to be an atheist or even a Christian? You made no choice in the beginning—you were born Muslim, so then you had no real choice about who you are and what you believe?

America is my country, though I do not think all we do is correct. I am a Christian first, an American second. Being an American does not commend me to God in any way. Christian does not equal American and vice versa. Wherever I live the Scripture commands me to be a good citizen. We do stand for freedom and an open society, and these are great things. I hate war, as anyone would, and I wish there weren't a reason for a war on terrorism. But there is, and we can pray that it will end soon and we can all live in peace.

Would the destruction of America solve Islam's problems? Would the destruction of Israel solve Islam's problems? Is not the problem sin and rebellion in the human heart? Isn't the human heart deceitful and desperately wicked, as the prophet said (see Jeremiah 17:9). Perhaps Muslims might feel superior and vindicated, if America and/or Israel should fall, but would that stop the warfare that constantly goes on within the "Muslim brotherhood"? The problem is a proud spirit and evil that lurks within—and it was for all this that Jesus died on the cross. Jesus died in our place, taking the death and judgment and hell upon Himself that we would have to bear, if we were to die unforgiven. Jesus was sacrificed instead of us; He atoned for the transgressions of those who believe in Him.

Over and above all that goes on in this crazy world, there is the reality of God. Let us seek Him, let us honor Him, let us worship Him, let us love Him. He has made this possible through our Lord Jesus Christ. Jesus said,

"Come to me, all who labor and are heavy laden, and I will give you rest. Take my yoke upon you, and learn from me; for I am gentle and lowly in heart, and you will find rest for your souls. For my yoke is easy, and my burden is light" (Matthew 11:28-30).

Kent Philpott
March 2002
Mill Valley, CA

Essay 9

Shame versus Guilt

There is a world of difference between a shamed-based culture and a guilt-based culture.

"Culture" can mean a whole nation, religion, tribe, clan, family, church, or any other similar entity.

As an example let us say that a Christian leader is found to be guilty of a sin, which then is made know to others.

The shame-based church, of which there are many, particularly among churches that tend toward legalism, and might be either a works-oriented or a grace-oriented church. The fallen Christian leader is an embarrassment to the church, maybe a wider grouping of churches, perhaps a whole denomination. This leader may be cast aside, fired, shunned, or any number of things might happen. This is known as "shooting the wounded" and is demonstrative of a shame orientation.

The guilt-based church with a fallen leader will not shoot the wounded but will take steps to bring healing and reconciliation. And this will work when the Christian leader acknowledges the sin and moves away from it, confesses his sin to God and man, and repents. If treatment or therapy is required, very well, but the fallen leader is restored.

The difference between a shame-based and a guilt-based church could not be greater.

Now then, let us change the scenario. Islam is founded on and produces a shame-based culture. For instance, if a young woman rejects an arranged marriage, she dishonors her family, clan, and tribe, indeed the religion of Islam itself. It falls to the family to restore honor, and this is very often accomplished by the killing of the young woman. The father, a brother, even a mother, will carry out this act. The young woman brought shame, and the only way to restore honor is murder. The murderer is not shamed but honored.

Or, to site another example, a member of the family or clan converts to another religious faith. Knowledge of this might be discovered and become widely known. To restore honor, the apostate must be killed. The murder covers the shame, and again, the murderer(s) are honored.

Or again, let us say a starving ten-year-old boy steals a loaf of bread at the town's market, is caught, and has his hand chopped off without anesthetic in the public square (common in Saudi Arabia), for honor to be restored to the community.

The above are examples of what may happen in a shame-based culture.

So too, in shame-based cultures there is a great deal of secrecy and silence. For instance, homosexuality is harshly condemned among Muslims, and a homosexual caught in the act may well be killed, depending on the country. At the same time, homosexuality is widely practiced, especially in Muslim-dominated countries, but it is concealed from public view. Shame only comes when forbidden acts are exposed. The sin of the act itself it not what brings shame; it is the exposure of the act that brings shame.

Consider a guilt-based culture, say an evangelical Bible-based church, which will probably view homosexual behavior to be sinful. If a case comes up in such a church, the sin does not tarnish the entire church community. The individual involved hopefully will receive appropriate ministry aimed at restoration and recovery.

THE BIBLE WAY

Most readers of the New Testament know that when Jesus was arrested and taken away to trial, Peter denied Jesus three times. Jesus even told Peter and the rest of the disciples that such would be the case (see Mark 14:26–31). It turned out just as Jesus had foretold (see Mark 14:66–72).

Peter thought he was so strong, but fear got the better of him. When the pressure came, Peter crumbled completely. After the third denial, Peter finally came to himself: "And he broke down and wept" (Mark 14:72).

The early church was not a shamed-based culture but a guilt-based culture. The chief apostle fell and did so publicly, and everyone who has ever read a Gospel knows this. Peter was not shunned and did not suffer violence; rather, he continued be the one who preached the first Christian sermon, which we find in Acts, chapter two, and upon whose name the

Roman church claimed to be founded.

Jesus Himself demonstrated for His Church the way things ought to be. We find a gripping and amazing story in the twenty-first chapter of John's Gospel. The scene is a beach beside the Sea of Galilee after Jesus' resurrection. It was a spring morning, and Peter, along with six other apostles, went out in a boat to fish but without success. Then at dawn the fishermen saw on the shore a stranger who told them where to cast their net. Immediately, the net was nearly bursting with fish. It was then Peter realized who the stranger was, so he jumped into the water and rushed to Jesus. Later on after the breakfast, which Jesus had prepared for the seven, Peter and Jesus took a stroll along the beach. As they walked, Jesus asked Peter three times if he loved Him. Three times Peter answered, "yes" and three times Jesus responded with, "Feed my sheep."

Peter denied Jesus three times. Jesus gave Peter the blessed opportunity to affirm his love for his Master three times. Jesus did not bring Peter's sin up to him; there was no need, since the Holy Spirit does this far better, and Peter was encouraged to continue to follow Him.

This is the great model for a guilt-based culture, which the Church must be if it is to be healthy. The legalists get in the way, however, and twist things to shame-based. This is what Islam has done, along with so many other religions, and certainly most of the Bible-based cults in Christianity have followed this pattern.

And it is to the legalists, those who are sinners as we all are, to whom I am reaching out with this essay—whether Muslim, Christian, or whatever.

Jesus died on the cross to cover sin, not shame. Biblical Christianity is guilt-based and thankfully so, since sin may be forgiven. The healthy church is not shamed by the acts of an individual. And most importantly, God delights in redeeming guilty sinners and erring Christians.

THE REAL PROBLEM

The real problem with a shame-based culture is that guilt is never dealt with but persists and often resurfaces as depression, anger, or self-hatred—maybe all of these.

Imagine the father who is forced to kill his daughter who refuses to marry a man she neither knows nor loves. The shame may be covered by the murder of the girl, or so it is assumed, but what about the conscience, the heart, or the mind of the family members? Guilt, a natural occurring brain function, remains. And there is no forgiveness.

A young boy or girl steals a loaf of bread, is caught, and brings shame upon the family and clan. Sharia Law demands a public amputation of a hand and/or a foot. What about the boy or girl, the family, the friends? What about the observers of the event or those who have the responsibility of carrying out the punishment? Everyone is traumatized, unless all these people are inoculated against such atrocities, which I suspect might be the case when a person is brought up in a shame-based culture.

I was a medic with the U.S. Air Force from 1961 to 1965. My unit was 2nd Casualty Staging Flight, which is based at Travis Air Force Base in Fairfield, California. For years my duty hours were from 5 PM to 8 PM. Many a green beret or ranger who had been wounded in Vietnam (starting in1963) would wonder down to my office late at night, and we would spend hours talking about what happened to them. It was known then as combat fatigue, and it was real. Not all had suffered actual bodily wounds. Many were listed as psychiatric on the flight manifest. Some had killed, raped, and maimed innocent civilians. They knew horrors such as I had never heard. My own brother, a combat engineer in Vietnam, came back emotionally wounded from experiences there and eventually committed suicide. With my college background in psychology and my newfound faith in Jesus, I was able to talk about forgiveness with traumatized young men. And for some, not many, the forgiveness found in Jesus Christ and His cross made all the difference.

Post-Traumatic Stress Disorder, or PTSD, can be deadly. Those who have experienced it have a high rate of suicide, become psychotic, and sometimes go off on murderous rampages. (The statistics are available by means of a Google search.)

I cannot help but wonder about the wrenching struggles many experience in Muslim cultures where the covering of shame is virtually mandated. Guilt does not go away. There it sits, eating away like a cancer deep in the interior. And this is why I emphasize the shed blood of Jesus in my witness to Muslim people.

At the conclusion of every morning service at our small Miller Avenue Baptist Church in Mill Valley, California, we observe the Lord's Supper. We do it because Jesus directed His Church, the Body of Christ, to do so. (There is no set frequency of observance.) We also do it because it is a wonderful presentation of the forgiveness that we have in the finished work of

Jesus, the Son of God. I conclude this essay with some of the passages we recite just prior to receiving the Bread and the Cup.

The Confessional:
"For there is no distinction: for all have sinned and fall short of the glory of God." Romans 3:23

The Jesus Prayer:
"Lord Jesus Christ, Son of God, have mercy on me, a sinner."

The Promise of acceptance and forgiveness
"If we confess our sins, he is faithful and just to forgive us our sins and to cleanse us from all unrighteousness." 1 John 1:9

Individual, silent prayer of confession

The Confirmation:
"There is therefore now no condemnation for those who are in Christ Jesus." Romans 8:1

The Assurance:
"Those whom he predestined he also called, and those whom he called he also justified, and those whom he justified he also glorified." Romans 8:30

Essay 10

Abrogation or Progressive Revelation?

Surah 2:106 of the Qur'an reads:

Such of Our revelations as We abrogate or cause to be forgotten, we bring (in place) one better or the like thereof. Knowest thou not that Allah is Able to do all things?" (from The Glorious Qur'an translation)

Another edition of the Qur'an, *The Holy Qur'an*, translated by Abdullah Yusuf Ali, Surah 2:106 reads slightly differently:

> None of our revelations
> Do We abrogate
> Or cause to be forgotten,
> But We substitute
> Something better or similar:
> Knowest thou not that God
> Hath power over all things?

Though the renderings differ, the meaning is obvious; earlier verses received by Muhammad were replaced by later verses. And abrogation, the replacing of doctrines, is of great interest.

Abrogation

Very early Muhammad received from Gabriel the message that the Jews and Christians, people of the Book as they were known, and who shared a similar origin with Muslims, were not counted as disbelievers.[1]

---

1 The exact process by which Muhammad received the recitations from Allah that eventually became the Qur'an, through the angel Gabriel, is unclear. Allah did not appear to Muhammad nor did Muhammad hear directly from Allah. The

First, from The *Glorious Qur'an*:

Lo! Those who believe (in that which is revealed unto thee, Muhammad), and those who are Jews, and Christians, and Sabaeans[2] – whoever believeth in Allah and the Last Day and doeth right – surely their reward is with their Lord, and there shall no fear come upon them neither shall they grieve.

Then from the Ali translation:

> Those who believe (in the Qur'an)
> And those who follow the Jewish (scriptures),
> And the Christians and the Sabians,
> Any who believe in God
> And the Last day,
> And work righteousness,
> Shall have their reward
> With their Lord: on them
> Shall be no fear, nor shall they grieve.

Despite the differences in the two editions of the Qur'an, it is plain that the Jews and Christians—People of the Book—were not counted as disbelievers by Muhammad.

But things changed, due to any number of reasons, but mostly because of opposition to Muhammad's preaching from both Jews and Christians. Thus was born the concept of abrogation, that is, the later truths replaced or superseded the earlier truths.

There are many examples of abrogation in the Qur'an. One is the oft-quoted axiom that there is no compulsion in religion. The first sentence of Surah 2:256 reads: "Let there be no compulsion in religion." But this was abrogated or changed such that Islam would later be required to be forced upon disbelievers. It is interesting to note that Islam means submission, and originally it was by choice not compulsion. That changed with the opposition Muhammad received, even in Mecca, and especially so in

---

intermediary, Gabriel, was either physically present, or Muhammad heard the angel's voice, or Muhammad's mind was "impressed" and such impressions were passed on to others. This last idea is more probable, since it appears that Muhammad would enter a trance state to receive the revelations from Gabriel.

2   There is no nation or tribe known today as the Sabaeans. Little is known of their history.

Medina. It became normative that disbelievers would either be forced to convert or pay taxes to their Muslim overlords. If not, only death remained as an option. This is clearly stated in Surah 47:4 (The Ali translation):

> Therefore, when ye meet
> The Unbelievers (in fight),
> Smite at their necks;[3]
> At length, when ye have
> Thoroughly subdued them,
> Bind a bond
> Firmly (on them): thereafter
> (Is the time for) either
> Generosity or ransom.

From The Glorious Qur'an is Surah 5:33:

The only reward of those who make war upon Allah and His messenger and strive after corruption in the land will be that they will be killed or crucified, or have their hands and feet on alternate sides cut off, or will be expelled out of the land. Such will be their degradation in the world, and in the Hereafter theirs will be an awful doom.

Of course, there are the Satanic Verses (about which Salmon Rushdie wrote), where Muhammad at first conceded that a particular Arab tribe's god and goddesses would be honored, but later, after receiving significant negative reaction from Muslim faithful, Muhammad reversed course and condemned the worship of the pagan deities. At one point Muhammad had compromised with a pagan Arab tribe, the Quraish, regarding their deities, Al Lat, Al Uzza, and Manat, and had said that he had received from Allah that these idols could be worshipped. While this news thrilled the Quraish, the Muslim faithful were quite unhappy about it. In time, the verses acknowledging the efficacy of the gods and goddess of the Quraish tribe were abrogated. Passages to look to on this matter are: Surahs 17:19–20, 22:52–53, and 53:19–20.

Muslims do not deny the practice of abrogation, but rather uphold it.

Muslims also see their religion as superseding or replacing Judaism

---

[3] "Smite at their necks" came to mean beheading.

Abrogation or Progressive Revelation?

and Christianity, as an intentional and natural progression ordained by Allah. Islam, Muslims believe, is the culmination of what is revealed in the Scripture, meaning the Old and New Testaments. Certainly, Christians claim the Old Testament to be inspired by the Creator God, while official Judaism rejects the New Testament in terms of it being revealed by the God of Abraham, Isaac, and Jacob.

Islam is not the only religion to regard their revelations to be the final message from God. This approach has been copied by many over the years, including the Mormons; in fact, Islam and Mormonism share an uncanny resemblance. In Mormonism you have an angel giving the book of Mormon on golden plates that present a new and improved truth that abrogates all that went before, especially referring to Biblical Christianity.

Progressive Revelation

Christians hold that the New Testament does not make much sense apart from the Old Testament. We see the prophecies of the Messiah sprinkled throughout the Hebrew Scripture, starting with Genesis 3:15:

> *I will put enmity between you and the woman,*
> *and between your offspring and her offspring;*
> *he shall bruise your head,*
> *and you shall bruise his heel.*

The woman Eve was a type extending on and pointing to Israel the nation, then Mary the mother of Jesus, then the Church. These entities are the "woman" of Genesis 3:15, and it has been understood in this manner down through the centuries. The offspring of the woman delivers a deathblow to Satan, the serpent, while the serpent merely bruises the offspring's heel. And that is how it worked out, just as Genesis said. The Apostle John much later wrote, "The reason the Son of God appeared was to destroy the works of the devil" (1 John 3:8b).

Then there is Psalm 22 where King David describes a man dying on a cross, and he wrote it around 1,000 years before the actual event took place. Not only that, but history tells us that the Greeks did not use crucifixion as a means of execution until many centuries after David wrote his Psalm. Then the Romans picked it up from the Greeks some centuries later.

The 22nd Psalm begins with words Jesus spoke while on the cross: "My God, my God, why have you forsaken me?" This forsakenness is the subject of Jesus' prayer in Gethsemane (see Mark 14:32–42). In verses 16 to 18 of Psalm 22 we find,

> *For dogs encompass me, a company of evil doers encircles me, they have pierced my hands and feet – I can count all my bones – they stare and gloat over me; they divide my garments among them, and for my clothing they cast lots.*

There is more from this Psalm that makes it clear David is depicting a man dying on a cross.

In the eighth century before Christ, the prophet Isaiah described the suffering servant of Israel who dies for sin as an atoning sacrifice to the holy God of Israel. Following are just a few verses from Isaiah, but the whole of the chapter, even parts of chapters 52 and 54, could be presented as well. Here is Isaiah 53:5–6:

> *But he was wounded for our transgressions; he was crushed for our iniquities, upon him was the chastisement that brought us peace, and with his stripes we are healed. All we like sheep have gone astray; we have turned every on to his own way; and the LORD has laid on him the iniquity of us all.*

Verse 9 of Isaiah 53 describes exactly what happened after Jesus' death on the cross: "And they made his grave with the wicked and with a rich man in his death, although he had done no violence, and there was no deceit in his mouth." Jesus died as a criminal yet was buried in a rich man's grave, that of one of the members of the elite Sanhedrin, Joseph of Arimathea.

Isaiah did more than speak of the suffering servant of Israel; he prophesied that the Messiah would be born of a virgin. The key verse is Isaiah 7:14: "Therefore the Lord himself will give you a sign. Behold, the virgin shall conceive and bear a son, and shall call his name Immanuel." Two key points are made in the verse. One, a virgin would conceive and give birth—"offspring"—(remember Genesis 3:15 and the offspring of the woman). And two, the child would be God. Immanuel means "God with us." There it is, the child is actually God become flesh. Here is how the Apostle John put it: "And the Word became flesh and dwelt among us" (John 1:14a). We note that in verse one of chapter one of John's Gospel he makes it clear that the "Word" is God.

Then the prophet Micah, long centuries before Jesus' day, described

His birthplace. "But you, O Bethlehem Ephrathah, who are too little to be among the clans of Judah, from you shall come forth for me, one who is to be ruler in Israel, whose origin is from of old, from ancient days" (Micah 5–2). And that is just where Jesus was born—Bethlehem. Almost hidden in the prophecy is the idea that the one born is from ancient days, meaning one with a long history.

There is Daniel's prophecy that describes the period of time when the Son of Man would appear. And also the prophet Malachi stating that there would be a forerunner announcing the coming of the Messiah, one crying in the wilderness to prepare the way for the arrival of that long promised Messiah. And it would be fulfilled when John the Baptist saw Jesus coming to be baptized in the Jordan River. John cried out, "Behold, the Lamb of God, who takes away the sin of the world" (John 1:29).

The point is that everything about Jesus, from who He is, what He did, when He did it, and what it meant was all outlined centuries before the events took place in real time.

The Distinction

Abrogation is utterly different from progressive revelation. In the Qur'an, changes in policy and understanding forced Gabriel, Allah, Muhammad, or someone, to change their mind. The Jews and Christians would be tolerated for only a few short years, until suddenly not tolerated anymore.

Progressive revelation is God beginning at one point and moving throughout history toward the end goal, His ultimate intention, which is to bring those made in His image, those whom He called to be His chosen people, to once again have perfect fellowship with Him in paradise.

The difference between Islam and Biblical Christianity could not be greater.

Two More Little Things:

*Works and Grace

Muslims depend on getting lots of points by performing rites and rituals so that they have a chance of going to paradise when they die. Stated another way, Islam is works-based. It all depends on what one does. The sure way to get to paradise is to die in violent jihad or maybe to build a mosque. In any case, it is chancy since Allah is a deceiver and might just lead one astray. Interestingly, one of the 99 names of Allah is Deceiver.

Going to heaven to be with Jesus forever depends on the grace of God that is freely given to lost sinners like me. I cannot earn it, achieve it, or work so very hard, even die a martyr—no, nothing at all I do will make it happen, as it all depends on God's love. "For God so loved the world, the he gave his only Son, that whoever believes in him should not perish but have eternal life" (John 3:16). And even the "believes" part is a gift, as Paul points out in Ephesians 2:8–9: "For by grace you have been saved through faith. And this is not your own doing, it is the gift of God, not a result of works, so that no one my boast."

*World Views

I do have to mention a second major difference between Islam and Christianity that involves the fundamental goals of the two religious systems.

Islam intends, as commanded by Allah in the Qur'an, to dominate the world. The state and the religion must be one under Shar'ia Law—this is the Muslim worldview. This is why Muslims claim Islam is the "religion of peace." Because, when Islam dominates, all enemies will be subdued, and there will be peace. This will be accomplished by whatever means necessary and is the reason for the horrors perpetrated by Muslims who take the Qur'an seriously.

Christianity has one goal this side of the return of Messiah Jesus, and that is summed up by Jesus Himself in Acts 1:8: "But you will receive power when the Holy Spirit has come upon you, and you will be my witnesses in Jerusalem and in all Judea and Samaria, and to the end of the earth."

Although there have been times when Christendom got it wrong and allied itself with military and political power—and forced conversions, as if such a thing were possible, Biblical Christianity is evangelical. True Christianity has always had its evangelicals from day one. By evangelical I mean all those, regardless of what group they belong to, who go about presenting the gospel of Jesus. Christians are to present the message of Christ, and the Holy Spirit does the rest. It is as Paul says in Romans 10:17: "So faith comes from hearing, and hearing through the word of Christ." Jesus, both who He is and what He did on the cross, is offered, simply preached, and those whom God has called will be convicted of their sin, the Holy Spirit will reveal Jesus as the Savior, and the miracle of conversion will take place.

The contrasts between Islam and Christianity are nearly endless, but this essay at least points out some of the more dramatic ones.

Essay 11

Eid Al-Adha: Who Has it Right?

Eid al-Adha, the great feast of Islam, also called the Day of the Sacrifice, falls on the 10th day of the last month of the lunar calendar. It comes during the Hajj pilgrimage festival, the fifth pillar of Islam, and is essentially a reenactment of Abraham's near sacrifice of his son, the Biblical account of which is found in Genesis chapter 22.

The essential Qur'anic story is found in the 37th chapter and verses 99 to 109. Quoted now from The Noble Qur'an:

99   He said, 'I am going towards my Lord; He will be my guide.
100   My Lord, bestow on me a right-acting child!'
101   And We gave him the good news of a forbearing boy.
102   When he was of an age to work with him, he said, 'My son, I have seen in a dream that I must sacrifice you. What do you think about this?' He said, 'Do as you are ordered, father. Allah willing, you will find me resolute.'
103   Then when they had both submitted and he had laid him face down on the ground,
104   We called out to him, 'Ibrahim!
105   You have fulfilled your vision. That is how We recompense good doers.
106   This was indeed a most manifest trial.
107   We ransomed him with a mighty sacrifice
108   and let the later people say of him:
109   'Peace be upon Ibrahim.'

It is plain that neither the names Isaac nor Ishmael are in the above text. Only Islamic sources and tradition provides names, some Ishmael, and some Isaac.

Abraham, the true Muslim, in absolute obedience and submission to

Allah, intends to sacrifice his son—Ishmael or Isaac. (To reiterate: Islamic scholars are divided on just who was to be sacrificed.) God intervenes and provides an animal to be sacrificed in place of the son. For Muslims the bottom line is that they are to be like Abraham and fully submit to Allah's commands.

THE BINDING OF ISAAC

In Genesis 22:1–19 of the Hebrew Scripture is the story of the sacrifice of Isaac. God instructs His obedient servant Abraham to take his son to the region of Moriah and there sacrifice him. Abraham called the place of the sacrifice "the LORD will provide" (verse 14). The writer in that same verse adds, "On the mountain of the LORD, it will be provided." Later on, in the Hebrew Scripture—Isaiah 2:3 and 30:29, Zechariah 8:3, and 2 Chronicles 3:1—we read that the temple is built on the "mountain of the LORD" or Moriah, the very mountain where Isaac was to be sacrificed.

For Judaism, the story of the obedience of Abraham is not much different from that of Islam, except that Islam does not focus on sacrifice but on obedience and submission to the will of Allah. For Judaism, much has to do with the actual location of the sacrifice, the temple mount where the temple of Solomon would be built and which therefore lays the ground for the whole sacrificial system we find in the Torah, especially Exodus and Leviticus.

THE RAM AS SUBSTITUTE

One of the areas on which Christians tend to agree is the reason for the Binding of Isaac (Abraham bound Isaac before placing him on the makeshift altar—Genesis 22:9). While Abraham was indeed obedient to God, and yes, the location was likely Jerusalem and maybe even where the temple was built more than a thousand years later, the real storyline for Christians has to do with what we call "substitutionary atonement."

What happened in our Genesis account? God told Abraham to take his son, his "only son Isaac" by the way, to a place far away and there kill him as a sacrifice. Abraham would have been familiar with animal sacrifice, as various forms of evidence demonstrate such was part of religious customs in Abraham's world. He did not hesitate and was about to go through with it when he was stopped cold. Here now is Genesis 22:11–14:

But the angel of the LORD called out to him from heaven and said,

EID AL-ADHA: WHO HAS IT RIGHT?

"Abraham, Abraham!" And he said, "Here I am."

He said, "Do not lay your hand on the boy or do anything to him, for now I know that you fear God, seeing you have not withheld your son, your only son, from me."

And Abraham lifted up his eyes and looked, and behold, behind him was a ram, caught in a thicket by his horns. And Abraham went and took the ram and offered it up as a burnt offering instead of his son.

So Abraham called the name of that place, "The LORD will provide"; as it is said to this day, "On the mount of the LORD it shall be provided."

In place of Isaac a substitute was provided for the sacrifice. The spilled blood and death of an animal was acceptable to God, and Isaac did not die.

It was a burnt offering, which meant that after the sacrificial animal was killed the remains were burned. A burnt offering is for covering or atoning for sin—substitutionary atonement.

GOD DID NOT SPARE HIS OWN SON

The New Testament is essentially about, perhaps only about, substitutionary atonement. Here God does not spare His only Son. The two verses below explain what I am trying to say.

For God so loved the world, that he gave his only son, that whoever believes in him should not perish but have eternal life (John 3:16).

He who did not spare his own Son but gave him up for us all... (Romans 8:32a).

"Gave" means giving up to death, and in the case of Jesus the Son, it is death on a cross, which is exactly what King David spoke of in Psalm 22, and also the Prophet Isaiah recounted in Isaiah 53. From the point of view of a Bible-believing Christian, it cannot be missed.

Who would or should have been given up to death? You and I, is the plain answer.

For the wages of sin in death, but the free gift of God is eternal life in Christ Jesus our Lord (Romans 6:23).

The God of the Bible, both Old and New Testaments, is a holy God who will not tolerate sin in His presence, thus the necessity for hell. And

I testify that I would not want to bring my load of sin into the presence of God, even if I could. No, I would much prefer hell.

But for reasons I do not fully understand, my Creator God loves me, and it is His desire that I should enjoy His fellowship forever. (Wow, it is beyond comprehension that He should act on my behalf since I helped send His only Son to die horribly on a criminal's cross!) Since I am a rotten sinner unable to do anything to atone for it myself, God provided "a ram caught in a thicket" (and rams do not get caught in thickets) to be bound and sacrificed in my place. This is the essence and the totality of it. We must then depend solely on the grace of a loving God.

How Could Islam and Judaism Get it Wrong?

Islam has no choice but to get it wrong, because the religion denies that Jesus even died on the cross. Salvation for Muslims is based on obedience to Allah, hopefully doing more good than bad.

Islam, as I mentioned above, is divided as to who was bound, Isaac or Ishmael. Many Muslims say Ishmael, because Arab tribes are thought to descend through Ishmael and Jews through Isaac, making Ishmael more of a father to the original Muslim world. The reason some Muslims say Isaac is because the Qur'an is not clear on the subject (see Qur'an 37:107).

Judaism sticks with Isaac since that is clearly attested in the Hebrew Bible. Christians stand with the same choice, but the Christian position of substitutionary atonement pointing to the ultimate substitute, Jesus, is unacceptable to official Judaism.

An Appeal

Let me state emphatically that one's position on this issue has eternal consequences. I know this is complex and mystifying, and the emotion of fear looms large, as one's whole identity is also placed into the mix. But we must see the larger picture, the only one that counts. Is Jesus our substitute, the One who took our sin upon Himself and freely and completely wipes out all our sin forever? This is the one and only true thing that counts, ultimately.

My appeal then is this: Find a time to be alone. Get on your knees and bow your head. Address God, Allah if you like, and ask Him whether Jesus died in your place. It is okay to do so; it is only reasonable that you do so. You have nothing to fear, nothing to lose, and everything to gain.

When you find yourself trusting solely in Jesus for salvation, I suggest you do the following:

1. Obtain a Bible and begin reading the Gospel of John, the fourth book in the New Testament.
2. Make a prayer list of concerns you have on your heart and in your mind. Find time to read your Bible and pray every day.
3. Find a group of those who believe in Jesus Christ as Lord and Savior and be in fellowship with them.
4. This group may be an organized church or not, but the main thing is that the Bible is taught and preached and that the Gospel message is proclaimed regularly and clearly.
5. This gathering of believers in Jesus may be large or small, the people may be young or old, rich or poor, educated or not.
6. This group should have an interest in communicating Jesus and His cross to others and be concerned about the poor and vulnerable around them.
7. This group, to be healthy and strong, should be able to disagree among themselves but keep focused on Jesus.
8. This group should identify with other Christians of whatever denomination and not see itself as the only correct and legitimate people of God.
9. It may take some time to find a Christian group with whom you will be comfortable but keep trying.

Essay 12

The Making of an Extremist

This essay is prompted by Patrick T. Dunleavy's book, *The Fertile Soil of Jihad: Terrorism's Prison Connection* (Washington D.C.: Potomac Books, 2011). In striking if not startling terms, Dunleavy describes how Islam in prison spreads in its many forms, including the Nation of Islam, the Dar-ul-Islam movement, and Prislam, a cultic form of Islam that sees its flock more as gang members than fervent converts. Muslim evangelism in prisons is growing, sponsored by both international and grass roots Islamic organizations. Its expansion over the years has been both phenomenal and disturbing. I am a firsthand witness to this.

My Prison Experience

During my thirty years as a volunteer at San Quentin State Prison in Marin County, California, I saw Islamic Da'wa (evangelism/recruitment) in action. While coaching the baseball team there for seventeen years, I sometimes arrived early and sat by a garden-type fountain (usually broken) that faced the building housing both the Jewish synagogue and the Muslim Mosque. Yes, a strange combination, but that is how it was and still is.

Over the course of five years, I listened to many sermons in English (unlike the sermons given in Arabic at the local mosque that I often visit), and I could easily follow along with the message. The messages by the imams were most often angry tirades about the persecution Muslims received over the centuries. Their hate speech frightened me from time to time, and I was tempted to speak to prison authorities about it, but I never did. (During that time, I did not understand as much about Islam as I should have.) In total, I probably heard ten or fifteen hours of outright expressions of rage and calls for revenge aimed at all that was non-Muslim.

Muslims began showing up to try out for the baseball team and the eight-man flag football team I formed. Every one of the Muslims were African Americans, and they were generally good players and reliable. One of them was my most trusted team member, a person I could rely on to tell what was going on with the team, if anything. We became friends, and the week after he was released from prison he came to our Sunday morning church service, stood before the congregation, and spoke to us for ten minutes; what he said was completely appropriate—and from a kind and generous spirit.

I correspond frequently on Facebook with this man who converted to Islam in prison, but I still do not know much about his background or how he became a Muslim. Recently, he dropped his Muslim name acquired in prison when he made his profession of faith, and he has gone back to his given name; I am not sure what that means, but I intend to speak with him about it.

Many African Americans have taken the path to Islam for several reasons. They find the doctrine compelling and the close-knit community welcoming, but there are also material benefits: they and their families on the outside often receive financial assistance, and a job and maybe a car will be waiting for the convert upon release from prison.

Dunleavy speaks about the selection of Islamic clergy for chaplain positions and the inadequate vetting process that allows imams with extremist views to enter the prison environment. Muslim evangelists able to find their way into prisons are almost always on the radical fringe.

The radicals begin their work little by little, and it is not just African Americans who are targeted. Hispanic and Anglo-American inmates are also pursued in Islam's prison outreach movement. To be counted as a Muslim in prison can be advantageous. There is a certain safety and special handling that often accompanies being in the prison's Muslim brotherhood. After all it is part of human nature to want to belong to a group that gives both purpose and meaning to one's life, no matter how misdirected that purpose is. Dunleavy's book speaks of the role of religion in the fertile soil of prison. They say there are no atheists in foxholes or prison cells, but theology and doctrine play a very minor role in conversions of convicts.

The irresistible draw is to be part of a world-wide brotherhood of like-minded people who have a compelling mission. And this Muslims certainly have. Here is a young convict with a messed up past and not much hope for the future, and along comes a group that offers great enticements and a sense of meaning. I am not surprised that many African Americans and other people in our world jump at the chance to be a part of it all.

THE WHYS

John Grisham, in his book, *Rogue Lawyer* (New York: Dell Books, 2015), gives a brief but accurate rendition of what drives African Americans, among others, into Islam. In the story line of the book the rogue lawyer is visiting his bodyguard's son who is in prison. Reading from page 109: "Young and black ... in for nonviolent drug offenses ... average sentence seven years ... three years later 60% are back ...convicted felons a branding they will never be able to shake ... ."

These are Grisham's words, but there is more, and my summary of the felon's situation is this: Filled with anger and a desire for revenge, with no job skills, no real education to build upon, no family to lean on for support, and no sense of wanting to build his own family; his only friends are ex-cons or partners in crime; he finds peace only in drugs and lives with an expectation that his life will be short. Grisham sums up with, "One million young black men now warehoused in decaying prisons, idling away the days at taxpayer expense."

I might add that now there are far more than just young blacks who fit this narration; growing numbers of Hispanics and whites are mixed in, and these numbers are growing. This is not an indictment, but it clears up any mystery of why Islam is growing in our prisons. If radical Islam feeds on the emotions of hate, anger, revenge, and alienation, this is a perfect storm condition for recruiting converts.

RECRUITMENT AND MOTIVATION

Anyone can be radicalized and end up committing horrible crimes as a result—and not only born Muslims. By radicalized I mean someone who goes to prison for burglary and ends up willing to die in violent jihad for the sake of Allah. This is far different from someone who goes to prison for burglary and learns how to perfect the art thereof. Anyone who kills in the name of God is an ideologue and has been radicalized.

If you are in one group, members of another group will likely be viewed as an enemy. It is safe to say that religion and politics are prime categories of people groupings and identity that have traditionally and historically produced real trouble. The Irish Republican Army is an example of political terrorism. ISIS and Al Qaeda are examples of religious terrorism.

Fighting back and getting revenge are compelling reasons for joining a group, though they may not be in the conscious mind at the point of recruitment. Almost all of us have these emotions in us, sometimes buried deep, and they are powerful motivators driving some to ignore or disregard the consequences of their actions. The promises made by the group for security, power, belonging, and meaning, even material wealth or outlandish notions such as seventy-two virgins awaiting the jihadist martyr hero, are all enough to blind the eye and stop the thinking.

It is nearly an everyday event now that some extremist blows himself or herself up in the hope of killing and maiming as many as possible; and is it all for the glory of Allah!

HARAM AND OTHER MOTIVATORS

Haram is Arabic for prohibited or forbidden.

There are two distinct world systems in the Muslim mind. There is Dar-ul-Islam (the world of Islam) and Dar-ul-Haram (the forbidden world). Much of the Western lifestyle is forbidden and seen as threatening the faith of a Muslim, particularly the young, through its seductions and enticement to things forbidden in the Qur'an. For the pious Muslim, it is a duty to attack the degradation of the West, especially American style degradation now that most of the country has embraced homosexuality. The excesses of contemporary civilizations are a motivator for those who want to live in the seventh century with Muhammad and his early companions.[1]

In my time, I have known Christians who were seduced by the immorality around them. This is the reality of our world, and it is unlikely to change much despite efforts to sanitize the culture. It is not a simple task to live for Jesus when all those around us demean it. (I live in the San Francisco Bay Area of California, so I know whereof I speak.) My experience

---

1   Those Muslims who want to return to the time when Islam first began are called Salafists. It comes from the Arabic word *salafi* meaning forefathers or the time of the forefathers.

is that Christians learn how to keep their footing regardless of the culture in which they are embedded. We understand that we are "in the world but not of the world." While not always easy, it is doable, since Christians have the indwelling Holy Spirit, the written Word of God, and hopefully a supportive church community.

What about the crusades? They were far away and long ago, and it is far from clear if the crusaders were "crusading" to lift up the name of Jesus. Mostly not. Nevertheless, Muslims use the battle cry "Crusades" to build anger toward Christians that will directed to acts of revenge; the charge need not be historically accurate.

What about colonialism? This is a major motivator for those who do not understand the development and expansion of nation states, most of which were not motivated by solid Christian and Biblical directives.

Oppression comes to mind. Muslims have been repressed; although, what people group has not been oppressed or repressed at some time in their history? This is too big a topic for this essay, but simply saying Muslims are being oppressed is enough of a trigger to set hearts and minds yearning for revenge. As I understand it, domination over Muslim countries, especially following World War I, flowed from the Western democracies.

But there is something else that may be a major if not the most important reason for Islam to be what it is today.

Fear of Failure in the Spiritual Marketplace

Extremists can be born out of a fear that Islam itself is inadequate to compete with other world religions, particularly Christianity.

One of the great contrasts with Christianity and Islam is that Islam's ultimate goal is to dominate the world—Dar-ul-Islam—to see to it that all people live under Sharia Law. No Muslim who really knows the Qur'an would deny this in private, yet some do publicly.

The goal of Christianity is to present the message of Jesus to all peoples on the planet. As I have heard it said, Christian evangelism is "one beggar telling another beggar where to find bread." And we know some will be convinced of their need of a Savior and turn to Jesus to save them from their sins. We also know that no amount of coercion, even slick persuasion, will yield a genuine new birth.

My sense of it is that only a small percentage of Muslims know much of what their religion teaches beyond the rituals, rites, pillars, and attendant cultural traditions. (This is also true of many in Christian churches. There is a difference between being religious and having true faith in Jesus as Savior and Lord.) I have met so many people who identify with Islam but are practical, if not actual, atheists. They will go through the motions, but their heads and hearts are empty. These people may be in danger, because the honor brigades in the mosques, the zealous and pious musclemen, will know who they are and will label them as "weak." Please note, I am not implying that this phenomenon exits only Muslim-dominated cultures. This exists wherever there is a mosque.

The message of Islam is not a comforting one. I am writing this essay after completing the basic content of this present book. A person, whether in prison or not, has a void in his or her life, a hunger and thirst, and will unconsciously attempt to fill it with something, somehow. Islam seeks to draw the thirsty with a false promise of water. I have pointed out the horrors that Allah has in store for non-Muslims and for Muslims as well. The Qur'an states that all Muslims will enter hellfire and will maybe escape it after a time. Allah is, after all, a deceiver and may lead even a faithful Muslim astray. Even those who die in violent jihad or who build a mosque have no real assurance of making it to paradise or escaping a temporary stay in hellfire. Allah's mercy and compassion are quite fickle, making the true message of Islam rather unattractive after all.

With any awareness of this reality, Muslims must fear that Islam is unable to compete in the spiritual marketplace of life. Today there are numerous former Muslims busy presenting Jesus and the message of the cross to Muslim communities. The Gospel is inescapable, and the draw is a Creator God who loves us and sent His Son to die in our place. Many Muslims are converting to Christ when Jesus is revealed through the faithful witness of believers and the drawing of the Holy Spirit. God chases down those whom He will. Conversion to Jesus is an event not a decision.

Death, and this is not merely physical but eternal death, is the end result of sin, yet the Christian has gone from death to life. Everyone dies, and then comes the judgment. On the cross, Jesus has taken our judgment upon Himself. We call this grace. We pray for it for our Muslim friends and neighbors. We do not pray for revenge or retaliation.

Essay 13

But, It Is Warfare!

War it is and of two kinds.

One Kind of War

Sadly, the killings go on daily. Who is waging this war? The jihadists—not all of Islam—are at war, or so we say. But some say we are in a real war with Islam itself. That is both accurate and inaccurate at the same time.

Islam's core doctrine is that Sharia Law must rule the world. There is no question about it, and any knowledgeable Muslim would concede this. While many if not most Muslims care little about Islam being the only true religion in the world, these moderates or progressives are not the shot-callers and have little real authority or power. We must therefore recognize to whom we are referring when we speak of war.

According to Islam, from the super pious to the moderates, the West is corrupt. What is to be done? While most Muslims want to live and let live, there is a sizable faction, perhaps as much as 5%, who are willing to go to battle. This 5% equates to around 500,000 dedicated warriors.

Another Kind of War

Christians are at war, too. In fact, we are called to take up the armor of God.

Finally, be strong in the Lord and in the strength of his might. Put on the whole armor of God, that you may be able to stand against the schemes of the devil (Ephesians 6:10–11).

For we do not wrestle against flesh and blood, but against the rulers, against the authorities, against the cosmic powers of this present darkness, against the spiritual forces of evil in the heavenly places (Ephesians 6:12).

Paul admits the existence of a war, but it is a spiritual war fought against an army mightier than any that humans could raise. He is referring to Satan and his minions. Fallen angels are the troops, and they possess spiritual power. C.S. Lewis used the term "hideous strength" in speaking of the ungodly power arrayed against the people who profess Jesus as Lord. If Christians think about this too long, we can become fearful, except that we recall 1 John 3:8: "The reason the Son of God appeared was to destroy the works of the devil."

John the Apostle wrote about the works of the devil and points out that the devil has been defeated—active yes, but nonetheless defeated, and in at least two ways. One, our sin—that which screams at us that we are no good and destined to live in hell forever—has been utterly removed, not in part but the whole, and it has been nailed to the cross. So our sin—all of it, past, present, and future—is wiped out, cleansed, washed away by the blood of the Lamb. Incredible, but a fact.

Then two, the enemy called death has been conquered. Not physical death, because we will all die unless Jesus returns before we physically die, but the real death is the eternal death.

Hellfire is very frequently found in the Qur'an, most often used as a threat and a warning, and thus hellfire is very present in the Muslim mind. On this point there is a connection with Biblical Christianity. There is a hell, most definitely, and it was created for the devil and his angels, for there must be a place apart for that which is unholy.

Physical death is but a moment in time; spiritual death, however, is eternal. It is plain which is the real enemy. It is no wonder why John 3:16 has for so many centuries been the one verse most Christians have memorized: "For God so loved the world, that he gave his only Son, that whoever believes in him should not perish but have eternal life."

It should be noted here, that in Islam Allah determines the moment and means of death. If a Muslim dies, it is the will of Allah. Biblical Christianity is far different. That we all die is plain enough, as we find in Hebrews 9:27–28:

"And just as it is appointed for man to die once, and after that comes the judgment, so Christ, having been offered once to bear the sins of many, will appear a second time, not to deal with sin but to save those who are eagerly waiting for him."

It is not the moment or means of death that God appoints but that death is a reality that comes with being human. Muslims may take comfort that death is in the hands of Allah, but Christians have the promise of being forgiven and having everlasting life based on what Jesus has already accomplished.

STILL ANOTHER KIND OF WAR-GAME

A convict told me years ago that to make it in prison you must have a mission. A mission, a cause, a reason for living, without which one might go crazy. Could it be that jihad becomes not just the means to accomplish the mission but the mission itself?

War-games are exciting to play. The secrecy, the codes, the manipulations, extortions, intimidations—war games. And the stakes are extremely high, making life all the more interesting.

When one has nothing or next to nothing, and the future looks bleak, and so many others seem to be living the good life, one stops caring and will bet everything on a cause, and Allah is the highest of all causes for pious Muslims. As General Patton is reported to have said, "Compared to war all else pales."

My point in this little aside is, maybe it is not religion that draws a religionist to the war.

THE WEAPONS OF OUR WARFARE

Back now to Ephesians chapter six and the weapons of the Christian's warfare, which are not bombs, knives, swords, or guns. Here is the list:

"Stand therefore having fastened on the belt of truth" (6:14a). Here truth is not a "what" but a "Who," and that Who is Jesus, who is the way, the truth and the life (see John 14:6).

"Having put on the breastplate of righteousness" (6:14b). Jesus Himself is our righteousness, we have none of our own but have His as a free gift.

"As shoes for your feet, having put on the readiness given by the gospel of peace" (6:15). The soldier stands secure knowing that he has no battle with God but is settled in the finished work of Jesus Christ on the cross. That war is over and there is peace.

"In all circumstances take up the shield of faith, with which you can

extinguish all the flaming darts of the evil one" (6:16). Since Satan's power over us has been nullified though the work of Jesus, we stand behind Him trusting in the triumphant Lamb of God.

"*And take the helmet of salvation*" (17a). The head, the most vulnerable part of the body, is totally protected in the salvation we have in Jesus, which cannot under any circumstance be taken from us. Our position in Christ is secure to all eternity, and even we ourselves cannot change that.

"*And the sword of the Spirit, which is the word of God*" (6:17b). "Word" is both the living and written word of God, Jesus Himself and the Scripture, the Bible from Genesis to Revelation. It is a sword, a spiritual sword, and it is sharper than any two-edged blade. The word is truth and there is great power in truth.

"*Praying at all times in the Spirit with all prayer and supplication*" (6:18a). We pray, not necessarily by rote, which is acceptable and a Biblical way to pray—I am thinking of the Lord's Prayer here—but saying to our heavenly Father what is on our heart and mind. The Christian is never alone; always walking with us is the Triune God, Father, Son, and Holy Spirit.

Oddly, or not, the equipment is not heavy and may be borne by the young and old, weak and strong.

This is our kind of war, one that has already been won. The only blow struck was inflicted a long time ago while Jesus was on Calvary.

Essay 14

Muslim Honor Brigades

Local Honor Brigades

In a nearby town is a tight knit community of Muslims, mostly from Thailand, Pakistan, and India, among others. Several years ago, a person who lived there asked me for help in moving her out of that area. In the process, I asked her why she was moving. She said it was to get away from the young toughs who were accosting women caught outside and not wearing a head covering. She described pushing and shoving, loud name calling, and more. These bands of young Muslim men and boys did this on a regular basis, and she was scared to death they would attack her, even though she was not a Muslim. A neighbor told her that she could be picked on, since they did not want non-Muslims in their community anyway.

What is this all about?

This sort of grouping of mostly young males is not officially sanctioned but is very real none-the-less. They can be found in every community where Muslims are the majority. Those who engage in these "brigades" are either real believers, convinced it is their duty to enforce Sharia law, or they follow along out of fear of being the object of the brigades themselves; they must show loyalty.

Based on my personal experience, I have found that a percentage of those born and raised Muslim do not believe in Allah at all. They are virtual atheists. They perform religious duties and rituals to be accepted by their Muslim families, friends, and communities. They would escape Islam if they could. But, so very often, they cannot.

How do I know this is so? By speaking with them in places away from the mosque. It is a sad thing, and I am surprised when they are interested in hearing about Jesus. Yet, to let this be known would certainly bring unwanted attention and concern from members of the brigade. It is not an easy thing to be a Muslim.

Being a Muslim is a full-time job. If one were to faithfully follow all the commands and prohibitions of that faith, there would be little time for anything else. The early Muslims did not live as most on the planet today have to live in order just to survive. With the necessity of earning a living, with families to look after, dwellings to keep up, and so on, there is not enough time and space to do all that is required to remain a virtuous Muslim. Therefore, many Muslims look to local, state, and national assistance.

Attending the local Sunni Mosque over the years, I observed week after week, that at least half of the congregation rushes in to be part of the service, if even for a minute or less. And their presence must be seen by either fellow Muslims, the imam, or even Allah. Those to impress are the local honor brigade plus the good angel who is sitting on the right shoulder taking notes and the jinn (demon) sitting on the left shoulder, who is also taking notes.

NATIONAL HONOR BRIGADES

Local honor brigades are hardly known to most people outside Muslim-dominated communities. This is not so in some countries, like England, where ninety-plus communities are blatantly only for Muslims, and in which Sharia law dominates. Local law enforcement agencies from the surrounding areas in England do not engage within the boundaries of those ghettos.

Operating largely under the radar in America are the large national organizations that function as honor brigades. These are collections of academics, activists, bloggers, and others, whose mission it is to protect and defend the honor of "true Islam." One of the familiar themes of such organizations is that Muslim violent extremists or terrorists do not represent Islam, and any person or organization that declares otherwise is guilty of "Islamophobia," which is the fear of Muslims.

Today the face of the honor brigade is seen in American academic institutions, non-profit organizations, and the media in general, who present a kind of soft propaganda aimed at silencing any criticism of Islam. Part of the mission of these groups is to discredit anyone who speaks or writes about Muslim extremism, intimating with the accusation of them having an irrational fear of Islam. Some of these Islamic groups are: The Council on American-Islamic Relations, known as CAIR, Muslim Advocates, the Muslim Public Affairs Council, and the Islamic Council of North America. These organizations use the words "racists," "bigots," "Islamaphobes," and other derogatory terms to describe those, like myself, who dare to present extremist Islam as it really is. And there is no question, despite the misrepresentations, that for these groups, their sole objective is to bring the entire world under subjection to Islamic Sharia law, meaning that all non-Muslims must either convert to Islam, be subservient to Muslims, or be killed.

These organizations are often funded by large and wealthy Muslim countries like Saudi Arabia, Qatar, and Iran. Yes, here Sunni and Shia branches of Islam will cooperate.

There is a Muslim Reform Movement whose mission is not to make excuses for Muslim terrorist activities, but to uphold an "Islam of grace." And there are some within this movement who want to have Islam seen as a religious faith along with others like Christianity, Hinduism, and Buddhism. However, this approach will not pacify or appease many Muslims, as they realize that at the core of Islam is the requirement that it must dominate and control and purge the world of opposing religions. This is seen in the sayings of the Muhammad of Medina, not the Muhammad of Mecca, who changed from being cooperative to being otherwise.

Islam and Islam only is the watchword of the honor brigades.

Essay 15

Sexual Repression in Islam

The title of this essay may seem a bit unusual, and a reader may wonder how I could know much about this subject. Therefore, let me describe an event that occurred around twenty years ago, at the time of the first Gulf War.

Young Men's Plight

My son, Vernon, was a military policeman in the U.S. Army, and he was stationed in Saudi Arabia even before the military action began. When it did, his unit's job was to move prisoners of war from the front battle lines to the rear. One of the processes was to take away from each prisoner, and they were all Muslims, what they had on their person, and that included their wallets. To their shock and surprise, these MPs found the photographs of these men's boyfriends—their lovers—within the wallets. Vern even mailed to me one of these photo envelopes, which had about six or seven photos of young Muslim men.

After contemplating what this all meant, it occurred to me that, due to the social circumstances in Muslim-dominated countries like Saudi Arabia, young men had little or no access to Muslim women. The older Muslim men, those with authority, wealth, and power, had multiple wives. Therefore, many of the young men had only one another. My opinion was, and is, that these guys were not truly homosexuals, as one might suppose.

It was about this time that I began to reach out to Muslims. I even, and on only a few rare occasions, was I able to ask Muslim men what this was all about. I would tell the story about my son Vern and the wallet contents. Every time, these guys flatly stated that they were ashamed about it but did admit that it was often so. They made sure that such was not the case here in America. And I believed them, to a point.

I then began to think about Muslim women in Muslim-dominated countries. In the process of writing my two books on Islam, *If Allah Wills* and *Islamic Studies*, and in talking with Muslim people following the Friday Jummah prayers, I saw, not so much heard, that relations between the males and females were carefully monitored and directed. And this is the case here in the good old USA. What then about Muslim-dominated countries?

WOMEN'S PLIGHT

What was revealed by means of conversations, was the extent of the troubled sexual relations that the young women also experienced. They were trapped by the men and separated from the outside world, and even if they did appear in public, they would have only their faces showing, often with a kind of net over their faces. For a period of two years, I conducted a kind of class situation at the church I pastor in Mill Valley and frequently invited guest speakers. Some of these were local Muslim leaders from both Sunni and Shiite mosques, in addition to former Muslims now believers in Jesus as Savior. And as best I could, I would ask these representatives to speak about how things were between Muslim men and women. There were some red faces and quite a bit of taqiyya(h), which means "permission to deceive." And this lying is even emulated, as made plain by one of Allah's 99 names, which is "The Greatest Deceiver."

A Muslim man can have four wives, and one can only surmise what might be taking place, as these wives are secluded and watched carefully. I have personal knowledge of a Muslim man, now elevated to the position of mufti, meaning one who can issue fatwas, who has four wives, but only one here in America. He travels year-round visiting three other wives and families who live in three different Muslim-majority countries.

REPRESSION TO PERVERSION

Sexual repression gives birth to sexual perversion, for men and for women. It is all undercover, and again, it is an embarrassment to most Muslim people. Normal human beings have a sexual drive, a need for sex. It is common to us all, and when this God given gift is denied or prevented from being expressed, irregular sexual activity should be expected.

During my thirty-five years at San Quentin Prison, which is about six miles away from where I am right now, I have encountered numbers of young men who have engaged in homosexual relationships either willingly or unwillingly. It is just a reality. For three years, I led a Bible study in the Protestant Chapel, and for fourteen years I visited inmates in their cells, either in West or North block. Then came eighteen years coaching the baseball team. This experience helped me understand the plight of some Muslim men and women.

The reason for the inclusion of this essay is to expose the reality of sexual repression for far too many young Muslim men and women.

Essay 15

Why the Taliban Enforces Strict Islamic Law

In the San Francisco Chronicle, September 24, 2021, was an article entitled "Strict punishment will return, says Taliban enforcer," and which prompted this essay. (That article was written by Kathy Gannon, an Associated Press writer.)

Highlighted in the Chronicle piece is this telling statement from Mullah Nooruddin Turabi, a Taliban leader in Afghanistan:

> "No one will tell us what our laws should be. We will follow Islam, and we will make our laws on the Quran."

Kathy Gannon's opening paragraph, datelined "Kabul" reads: "One of the founders of the Taliban and the chief enforcer of its harsh interpretation of Islamic law when they last ruled Afghanistan said the hard-line movement will once again carry out executions and amputations of hands, though perhaps not in public."

What is this all about?

Perhaps Fear is the Answer?

The Taliban must eliminate opposition and secure their power base, and harsh measures are meant to ensure compliance across the board. Losing a hand is a typical punishment, and losing a hand usually means losing a foot, too—right hand cut off, left foot cut off is the norm or the reverse. Execution is also likely by having one's head removed. All these measures that Westerners see as extreme are indeed fear-inducing for the potential transgressor but also demonstrate the Taliban's fear of losing control.

The executioner must comply, or he also could lose that hand or head. In Muslim-dominated nations, fear is the norm.

Why the Taliban Enforces Strict Islamic Law 91

Perhaps ensuring faithful Islamic compliance may be an answer

As I have mentioned in other essays found here is the reality that, if given the freedom, there would not be the near universal attendance at the mosques or giving of the Zakat, or almsgiving. Eyes are watching, and they might belong to a member of an honor brigade or simply one's neighbors, even family members. Islam is much less a heart focused faith than an action faith—what one does or does not do.

Perhaps fear of losing adherents to other faiths, especially Christianity

For decades, even centuries past, there have been large numbers of Muslims turning to Christ as Savior. Sometimes they remain in Muslim communities, even attending Jummah prayer on Fridays and giving the Zakat, with the women wearing the hijab or even the full burka. Where possible, in places where there is not a dominating Muslim community, those who have found salvation in Jesus Christ will join Christian congregations. (There are growing numbers of these in various parts of the world.)

Perhaps fear of being cast into hell-fire

In today's San Francisco Chronicle (November 17, 2021) is an article titled "Islamic State suicide bombers hit capital city," and the country is Uganda. Uganda's Muslim population is 14% of the nation's 44 million people, which is mostly Christian. The Muslims believe it is their duty to kill all non-Muslims, especially since doing so increases their chances of avoiding hellfire.

Muslims do not have the security of salvation that Christians do. When the new birth takes place, that incredible moment of salvation, of being indwelt by the Holy Spirit, we know that the greatest gift has been given to us through the grace of our Lord. It is a done deal, despite times of discouragement, failures, and doubting. Instead of this assurance is the never-ending effort to prove oneself a true Muslim.

In Muslim publications or when Muhammad's name is spoken, such will be followed with "Peace Be Upon Him." When Muhammad's name appears in print there will be PBUM, which is short for Peace Be Upon Him. Not even Muhammad is assured of being in Paradise, thus PBUM when either his name appears in print or is spoken. When questioned about the reason for this, most Muslims say that it is simply a way of honoring Muhammad. But that is a clean-up, a fabrication, since the literature is clear that no Muslim is assured of going to paradise when they die. Only the most zealous, the most faithful, the most dedicated Muslims have a hope of evading hellfire. Even dying as a martyr while blowing up non-Muslims may not be enough but is at least possible.

(Let me recommend my book, *Islamic Studies*, which deals with this issue more completely.)

Perhaps fear of not being strict enough

The Taliban in Afghanistan, now in the Fall of 2021, have as their fiercest enemy the Islamic State, which is more zealous for their religion than even the Taliban, if that is possible. And this is proven by harsh, barbaric enforcement of Islamic Sharia Law.

In the previous section of this essay, I mentioned Uganda and the bombings of innocent civilians due to no other reason than they are not Muslims. The suicide bombers are showing their zeal for Allah in the desperate hope they will be in paradise when they die, and they hope to die while murdering non-Muslims. Strict and very strict they are, all fear motivated.

How very far from this are the words of Jesus as found in the Sermon on the Mount. Here is the account:

> *"You have heard that it was said, 'You shall love your neighbor and hate your enemy.' But I say to you, Love your enemies and pray for those who persecute you, so that you may be sons of your Father who is in heaven." Matthew 5:43-45*

Perhaps the ever-ongoing fear is what the angels are recording

On the right shoulder of every Muslim is a good angel who is recording all the good deeds being performed. On the left shoulder of every Muslim is a bad angel who is recording all the bad deeds being performed.

The good deeds must outweigh the bad deeds or into hellfire one is cast. How scary! To the best of my knowledge, the thoughts in the head and the feelings in the heart are not recorded. I may be wrong about this though.

Why the Taliban Enforces Strict Islamic Law   93

Perhaps the fear of the daily activity of evil spirits dominates the life of Muslim people

During the night, when one is asleep, demons or evil spirits may enter in via the nose. Thus, every Muslim is to snort several times upon awaking to dislodge and dispel these spiritual critters. And these horrid spirits rule in hellfire and exist to torment those who have not walked the line carefully enough. One never knows where one stands.

Concluding remarks

In the eighth chapter of John's Gospel, Jesus addresses religious zealots who are seeking to have Him put to death. He said to them, "You are of your father the devil, and your will is to do your father's desires. He was a murderer from the beginning, and does not stand in the truth, because there is no truth in him" (John 8:44).

I am reminded of the first essay in this book entitled, "Who is Muhammad's Gabriel?" There I state that Gabriel is a demon and thus Allah is Satan. I am committed to stating this, so that by God's grace some Muslim people may be open to Jesus and be saved from sin and hell. As Christians we must be bold enough to proclaim Jesus, though it is a risky thing to do, considering what is going on worldwide and not only with the Taliban, the Islamic State, and other Muslim groupings.

We, in fulfilling the Great Commission to preach the love of our Lord Jesus Christ to all the peoples of the world, must reach out to Muslims who are loved of God and for whom Jesus went to the cross.

End Note

I Am Not Anti-Muslim

I am not anti-Muslim nor am I Islamophobic. I am a Christian pastor, and my calling and work is to reach out to those who are not trusting in Jesus as their Lord and Savior. I am hoping to fulfill the command of my Lord Jesus to preach His Word to all that I can.

Muslims will do the same to all those who are not Muslim. Some Muslims will present their message and leave it at that. Others will subjugate others and demand their conversion, and if not, death could follow. What a difference between the Muslim witness and the Christian witness as Jesus demonstrated it.

Almost twenty years ago, I had the sense that God was calling me to reach out to Muslim people. That impression came to me when coaching high school freshman baseball with two Muslim players on the team. They were great kids, and I became acquainted with their parents, and so then I began to pray for them that they would find Jesus. Then followed the essays and articles and finally whole books, all written with the purpose of reaching out to Muslims.

The next step was a two-year long television series with Imam Abu Qadir Al-Amin, head of a Sunni Mosque in San Francisco. For two years, we "debated," rather "discussed" key topics. This series is still available and can be found by going to milleravenuechurch.org/watch-our-tv-shows.

While I am not anti-Muslim, I am against forced Islamism. Islamism is an extremist ideology that intends to convert the world and all its peoples to Islam, so that it will be governed by Sharia law. Though those who move in this direction are not a substantial majority, still it has captured enough of the faithful to make things dangerous.

Indeed, the true Muslim is obligated to work to destroy that which stands in the way of Islam dominating the entire world, and by any means. To kill in the name of Allah is not only accepted but emulated by far too many extremists. These jihadists do not see themselves as extremists but see others who are not striving mightily to convert the world's people to Islam as being weak, misled, and subject to elimination.

This is tragic in two ways. One, there is no peace and pleasure in living in the world, rather strife and conflict is constant. Two, Muslim people are being fed a false salvation. There is no heaven waiting for the Muslim, only judgment and everlasting separation from God. Herein are the reasons for the writing and publication of this book. It is our effort to reach out to Muslim people, for they are people for whom our Lord Jesus Christ died, rose again, and will one day return to usher in eternity. May peace be upon Muslims the world over.

www.ingramcontent.com/pod-product-compliance
Lightning Source LLC
Chambersburg PA
CBHW030003050426
42451CB00006B/99